# Me, not you

# Me, not you

## The trouble with mainstream feminism

Alison Phipps

Manchester University Press

Published by Manchester University Press
Altrincham Street, Manchester M1 7JA
www.manchesteruniversitypress.co.uk

British Library Cataloguing-in-Publication Data
A catalogue record for this book is available from the British Library

ISBN 978 1 5261 4717 2 hardback

First published 2020

Typeset by Servis Filmsetting Ltd, Stockport, Cheshire
Printed in Great Britain by Bell and Bain Ltd, Glasgow

# Contents

# Acknowledgements

I want to give heartfelt thanks to the many women I have collaborated with in my research on sexual violence: gathering data, developing ideas, trying to change cultures that are almost impossibly resistant to change. Liz McDonnell and Jess Taylor are dear colleagues and even dearer friends: facing challenges is much easier when you do it together. There is a reason why the acronym for our project Changing University Cultures is CHUCL – when doing a difficult job, a bit of levity goes a long way. Thanks also to Vanita Sundaram, Pam Alldred, Naaz Rashid, Gemma North, Gillian Love, Susuana Amoah, Erin Shannon, Tiffany Page and Isabel Young. There are many more who have facilitated my scholarship and influenced my thinking, for which I am very grateful.

There are too many other comrades and teachers to mention, and if I try to write a comprehensive list there will always be people left out. So I am just going to name a handful of women who have inspired me: Mariame Kaba, Sara Ahmed, Molly Smith and Juno Mac. Thank you for challenging me with your words and works, whether you meant to or not. Thanks to the many trans people and sex workers on Twitter, the majority of whom do not even feel safe enough to use their real names, who have reached out to me and shared experiences and ideas. Thanks to my Sussex colleagues and comrades in the fight for a trans-inclusive feminist academia: Hannah Mason-Bish, Lizzie Seal, Marie Hutton and Claire Annesley, to name a few. Thanks to my students and especially those on the Gender Studies MA, who have taught me something new during every one of the last sixteen years. Special thanks to Patrick Strudwick, my old friend and partner in crime, who stops me being completely cynical about the media and who I still feel privileged to know. Little did we know that our shared travels through Manchester's gay village in the mid-1990s would endure in political form.

This book could not have been written without Jan. It could not have been written without Caitlin and Johann, even though (and because) they are young enough to be blissfully unaware of most of the issues it covers. It has also been built on the labour of others who help with my life-making including (but not restricted to) Becky, Sarah, Sheena, my Mum and Dad, and the many women (and a few people of other genders) who take care of my children while I work. The soundtrack (of course) has been provided by Prince. Sussex University has given me time and resources, amazing colleagues and the freedom to follow my own scholarly path. Parts of this manuscript have been published in earlier forms, in the journals

*Feminist Formations, Feminist Theory, Gender and Education, Journal of International Women's Studies* and *Soundings*. I thank these publications heartily for supporting and publishing my work.

Manchester University Press has been wonderful, and especially Tom Dark who has been supportive, encouraging and responsive: everything I could have wanted in an editor. Thanks also to Rob Byron, Lianne Slavin, Chris Hart and Andrew Kirk, and to Tanya Izzard for the index. I would like to thank the three anonymous reviewers who commented on the proposal and manuscript so generously and constructively. Any errors that remain are entirely my own.

This book is dedicated to all the amazing Black feminists who have spent their time and energy educating white feminists about white feminism, while also developing the rich ideas and politics which are central to my analysis. In grateful recognition of their labour, I am donating all royalties I receive to projects by and/or for Black women, in the UK and overseas, which focus on sexual violence. These include, but are not restricted to, Black Women's Rape Action Project, Imkaan, Sistah Space and Southall Black Sisters in England; Shakti Women's Aid in Scotland; BAWSO in Wales; Black Women's Blueprint, Incite, and Survived and Punished in the US; the Mirabel Centre in Nigeria; the Survivors Fund in Rwanda; Thohoyandou Victim Empowerment Programme in South Africa; Lawanci in South Sudan; and The Consent Workshop in Canada, Ghana, Nigeria, and Saint Vincent and the Grenadines.

# Introduction

In November 2017 the Alianza Nacional de Campesinas, representing 700,000 female farmworkers and women in farmworker families across the US, wrote a letter of solidarity to the Hollywood women at the centre of #MeToo. 'We do not work under bright stage lights or on the big screen', the letter said. 'We work in the shadows of society in isolated fields and packinghouses that are out of sight and out of mind.' Nevertheless, it continued, 'we believe and stand with you'. The question left unasked, taken up in discussions in the days that followed, was 'will you believe and stand with *us*?'

This question inspired the Time's Up initiative, a legal defence fund to help women in all industries fight sexual harassment. The first meeting was held at the home of actor Jessica Chastain – other white actors involved included Reese Witherspoon, Natalie Portman, Nicole Kidman, Amber Tamblyn, Jennifer Aniston and Margot Robbie. But women of colour were also at the forefront from the start. The founders of Time's Up included National Women's Law Center president Fatima Goss Graves, producer Shonda Rhimes, actors Rashida Jones, America Ferrara, Eva Longoria, Lena Waithe and Kerry Washington, and director Ava DuVernay. Its first CEO was the former Atlanta city councilwoman and WNBA president Lisa Borders. In 2018 Time's Up awarded $750,000 in grants to 18 organisations across the US supporting low-wage workers.

The profile of women of colour in such a mainstream initiative made Time's Up a departure from the norm. Nevertheless, it was criticised for being an 'exclusive club' and concentrating too much on white celebrities. It was also accused of using activists of colour as window dressing: for instance, at the 2018 Golden Globes, when eight white Hollywood stars each took an activist (including #MeToo founder Tarana Burke and Alianza Nacional de Campesinas president Mónica Ramírez) as their 'plus ones'. Time's Up occupies a complex position in a feminist mainstream dominated by white and privileged women. Even when women of colour are in leadership roles, the pull of whiteness is strong.

This is the trouble with mainstream feminism, encapsulated in the title of my book: 'Me, Not You'. This is, of course, a play on #MeToo. The #MeToo movement, started as a programme of work by Black feminist and civil rights activist Tarana Burke in 2006, went viral as a hashtag eleven years later after a tweet by white actor Alyssa Milano. And mainstream movements such as #MeToo have often built on and co-opted the work of women of colour, while <u>refusing to learn from them or centre their concerns.</u> Far too often the message is not 'Me, Too' but 'Me, Not You'. And, as I will write, this is not just a lack of solidarity. Privileged white women also sacrifice more marginalised people to achieve our aims, or even define them as enemies when they get in our way.

#MeToo is a movement about sexual violence, most of which is perpetrated by cisgender men. This book is also about violence – especially the violence we can do in the name of fighting sexual violence. When I say 'we', I mainly mean white women and white feminists. This book is addressed to my fellow white feminists; although it is dedicated to Black feminists, they will not need to read it.[1] For feminists of colour, the arguments I make here will probably be nothing new (and I hope this book will help ease the burden of constantly having to explain whiteness to white women).[2]

'we'

The 'Me' in the book's title also refers to me, a white feminist writing about white feminism. Some of the views I write about I have previously held; some of the dynamics I write about I have participated in myself (and might again in future, despite my best intentions). I am ambivalent about writing about whiteness: I am concerned, as some readers might also be, that in critiquing whiteness from within, I am trying to absolve myself of my own. I am worried that I am trying to be one of the 'good white people', who perform what feminist scholar Sara Ahmed calls a 'whiteness that is anxious about itself' and see that as anti-racist action.[3]

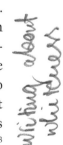 writing about whiteness

And deep down, that might be the case. Whiteness is wily: white supremacy is so embedded in our psyches that we end up doing it even while we claim (and believe) it is what we oppose. You are entitled – even invited – to make up your own minds about my motivations. But regardless of why you think I have written it, I hope you find something in this book of value. And if not, I am happy to be told I am wrong: knowledge is always partial, and we learn through dialogue with one another.

My analysis of mainstream feminism comes from fifteen years of research on, and activism around, sexual violence.[4] I am a white academic in this field, with all the privileges that entails. But my experience of it has been ambivalent and complex. I experience class anxiety in academia. My politics tend to differ from those of many other scholars and activists in my area, as well as (in other ways) from those of my family of origin. I am what Sara Ahmed would call a 'willful child': I do not fit in.[5] I am also a queer woman with non-paradigm experiences of sexual trauma. To understand all these things, I have repeatedly turned to the words and actions of Black feminists and other feminists of colour, trans women and sex workers (and women who fit two or more of these categories). Their ideas are what Ahmed would call my feminist bricks – it has been my privilege to spread some mortar between them.[6]

## What is 'mainstream feminism'?

This is a book about mainstream feminism. And by this, I mean mostly Anglo-American public feminism. This includes media feminism (and some forms of social media feminism) or what media scholar Sarah Banet-Weiser has called 'popular feminism': the feminist ideas and politics that circulate on mainstream platforms.[7] It also includes institutional feminism, corporate feminism and policy feminism: the feminism that tends to dominate in universities, government bodies, private companies and international NGOs. This is not a cohesive and unified movement, but it has clear directions and effects. In other texts, it has been called 'neoliberal feminism', 'lean-in' feminism and 'feminism for the 1%'.[8] This is because it wants power *within* the existing system, rather than an end to the status quo.

Mainstream feminism, exemplified by campaigns such as #MeToo, tends to set the agenda for parliamentary politics, institutional reform and corporate equality work. It tends to be highly visible internationally, because Western media forms are dominant across the globe. This profile and influence are the reasons why it is important to critique. But this mainstream movement is by no means the whole of feminist politics. I am aware that defining 'feminism' as white and privileged risks (re)constituting it as such, and I do not want to erase the fundamental contributions of feminists of colour. A founding assumption of this book is that the mainstream Anglo-American movement is often taken to represent feminism, when in fact it does not.

White and privileged women dominate mainstream feminism. These demographics shape the movement's politics, but are perhaps partially hidden by monikers such as 'neoliberal feminism', 'popular feminism' and the rest. In contrast, this book centres race, giving an additional reading of the movement at a time when white supremacy is being violently reasserted. There is already increasing discussion of 'white feminism', used to denote a feminism that ignores the ideas and struggles of women of colour. This book is based on the concept of *political whiteness*, which describes a set of values, orientations and behaviours that go deeper than that. These include narcissism, alertness to threat and an accompanying will to power. And perhaps most crucially, they characterise mainstream feminism *and* other politics dominated by privileged white people. They link movements such as #MeToo with the backlashes against them. And they link more reactionary forms of white feminism with the far right.

Political whiteness tends to be visibly enacted by privileged white people (but can cross class boundaries), and can also be enacted by people of colour because it describes a relationship to white supremacist systems rather than an identity *per se*. It is produced by the interaction between supremacy and victimhood: the latter includes the genuine victimisation at the centre of #MeToo and similar movements, and the imagined victimhood of misogynist, racist and other reactionary politics. I am not denying that mainstream feminism is rooted in real experiences of oppression and trauma. I am not saying that these experiences do not deserve to be taken seriously. But I am asking: how are these experiences politicised, and what do they do?

## Sexual violence in the intersections

My analysis of mainstream feminism is grounded in the principle of intersectionality. Developed by Kimberlé Crenshaw and other Black feminist scholars, this refers to the complex relationships that make up our social world[9] – relationships between categories such as race, class and gender, and between the associated oppressions of racism, classism and sexism. These are produced by intersecting systems: heteropatriarchy, racial capitalism and colonialism.

Patriarchy refers to the domination of women by men. This pre-dates capitalism (at least in the West), but capitalism embedded it by separating production and reproduction and making women responsible for the latter. Capitalism relies on social reproduction – creation of and care for human life – but doesn't want to foot the bill. Historically, white bourgeois homemakers were confined, unpaid, to the private sphere. Working women have been (and are) over-represented in the low-status and low-paid caring professions which also reproduce human life. And even if they are family breadwinners, women perform the bulk of domestic

*capitalism*

Colonialism / Racial capitalism

labour with little or no help from capital. Because we are seen as hardwired to care, as sociologist Maria Mies argues, our labour is exploited as if it is a 'natural' resource.[10] Women's work is not viewed as real work: it exists in the realm of 'love', not money. This is how capitalist patriarchy constructs gender.

Capitalist patriarchy is heteropatriarchy: it relies on the heterosexual nuclear family as an economic and reproductive unit. And as capitalism began to expand from the fifteenth century onwards, European colonialism and settler-colonialism exported this model of social organisation into most of the world. Common lands were subdivided into family plots; colonised people were defined as 'less-than-human' because they did not conform to the bourgeois nuclear family and its gendered separation of roles. Capitalism also was and is racial capitalism. It is built on the appropriation of Indigenous lands, enslavement of populations, and the ongoing exploitation of people of colour (women especially) as 'expendable' units of production and both biological and social reproduction.[11]

Racial capitalism does not just create inequality based on categories such as class, race, gender, disability, age and nation – it *relies* on it. To maintain a stratified system, to ensure that the economically privileged can monopolise resources, some people must be relegated to marginalised economic or reproductive roles. Others must be placed outside the system completely – stripped of their humanity, to be dispossessed and eventually done away with.

## Introduction

Violence against women is a pivot for the intersecting systems of heteropatriarchy, racial capitalism and colonialism. It results from the tussle for material and emotional resources, between commodity production and the reproduction of human life. Men's domination of women, essential to social reproduction, is achieved through violence and the threat of it: at home, in the workplace and on the streets. Racial capitalist development relied on forced reproduction via the rape of enslaved women, and coerced reproduction via the expectation that women in general would create and care for the workforce.[12] The 'primitive accumulation' of racial capitalism violently dispossessed women of land, resources and power to put them under men's control, making them more vulnerable to violence (and this continues in neo-colonial contexts).[13] Sexual violence is a form of terrorism that supports economic expansion. It kept (and keeps) conquered, enslaved and dispossessed populations in line.

But terror can also be generated through maiming and killing men of colour and impoverished white men accused of raping bourgeois white women. And it is this fact that mainstream feminist movements tend to minimise or forget. In colonial Australia, rape was a 'violation of female purity' punishable by death – politicians insisted that this was necessary to keep both Indigenous men and 'disreputable' white men under control. The story of the 'white woman of Gippsland', said to have been held against her will by Kurnai people in the 1840s, justified further brutalisation and dispossession of Indigenous Australian communities that had already been brutalised and dispossessed.[14] Following Lincoln's 1863 Emancipation Proclamation, white Americans used lynchings to terrorise and control free Black people. Rape of a white woman was one of the most common pretexts. And murder could escalate to massacre. In 1921 between 100 and 300 Black people in Greenwood, Tulsa, were killed by white mobs in a matter of hours after a Black man was falsely accused of raping a white woman in an elevator.[15]

A key premise of this book is that acts, threats *and allegations* of sexual violence are all tools of oppression. Sexual violence is terror; so is the way it is tackled and policed. And (white) 'women's safety' is used to justify violence against marginalised communities. This is a challenge for mainstream feminist movements against sexual violence, which are dominated by bourgeois white women.

This leads to the other key premise of this book: being a victim and being a perpetrator are not mutually exclusive. Bourgeois white women can be victims of sexual violence, but we are also perpetrators of race and class supremacy. Supremacy is expressed in the 'care chains' through which we exploit poorer women, often migrants and women of colour, to do the labour of social reproduction while we do more lucrative work. And it is expressed in the violence done in the name of 'protecting' us from violence, legitimating the hyper-exploitation and genocide of communities of colour.

White women's 'protection' is also at the forefront in a world moving rapidly to the right. 'White power', in the form of ideological fascism, border regimes and hoarding of resources, is being reasserted in response to economic and ecological crisis. And the difficult and painful questions this raises for mainstream feminism are at the heart of this book. While I do not hope or pretend to answer all of them, I hope this text might be a companion for other white women who, like me, are interested in doing their feminism differently. If that is you, please read on.

Christine Blasey Ford

## Chapter 1

# Gender in a right-moving world

The cover of *Time* magazine on 15 October 2018 was an illustration of Dr Christine Blasey Ford.[1] Artist John Mavroudis created it, using phrases from Ford's testimony to the Senate Judiciary Committee hearings on Brett Kavanaugh's confirmation to the US Supreme Court. These phrases were arranged into a striking image of Ford taking the oath. On her forehead is written 'seared into my memory'. This is how she described her experience, at the age of 15, of sexual assault by Justice Kavanaugh. It had happened, Ford said, at a small gathering of young people in the Bethesda/Chevy Chase area of Maryland. In an upstairs bedroom, Kavanaugh had climbed on top of her and tried to remove her clothes. She tried to yell for help. When she did, he put his hand over her mouth. 'This was what terrified me the most,' she said, 'and has had the most lasting impact on my life. It was hard for me to breathe, and I thought that Brett was accidentally going to kill me.'

In front of a panel of eleven Republicans (all men) and ten Democrats (mostly men), Ford recounted how the

assault had drastically altered her life. While remodel-
ling the house she shared with her husband she had
insisted on a second front door – a potential escape
route. As she had explained why she needed one, she
had described the assault to her husband in detail. She
recalled saying at the time that 'the boy who assaulted
me could someday be on the U.S. Supreme Court'. As
a survivor of sexual violence, this phrase rings in my
ears: it represents the right of powerful men to abuse
women with impunity.

It was also clear, during the hearings, that impunity
was what Kavanaugh and his supporters expected. His
demeanour during his testimony was widely contrasted
with Ford's – an image, circulated on social media,
showed him snarling as he shouted into a microphone.
He shouted a lot, in a long and irate speech in which he
called the process a 'national disgrace' and a 'grotesque
and coordinated character assassination' fuelled by
'anger about President Trump' and 'revenge on behalf
of the Clintons'. He seemed like a man accustomed to
getting his way.

And get it he did. Brett Kavanaugh was eventually confirmed as an Associate Justice of the Supreme
Court, after a perfunctory delay. But Christine Blasey
Ford's actions inspired an international wave of support. The hashtag #WhyIDidntReport trended on social
media. Tarana Burke and other leaders of #MeToo published an open letter of solidarity, and another one
was signed by more than 200 alumnae of Ford's high
school. Ford was nominated for the John F. Kennedy

Anita Hill

Profile in Courage Award, named 'person of the year' by the anti-sexual-violence group Raliance, and short-listed for person of the year by *Time*.

Ford was also compared to Professor Anita Hill, whose 1991 testimony during Justice Clarence Thomas's Supreme Court nomination hearings sparked a national discussion about sexual harassment. Hill accused Justice Thomas of repeatedly making unwanted advances towards her when she was his employee, first at the Education Department and later at the Equal Employment Opportunity Commission. She also said he would often talk about sex in detail at work, describing pornography he had watched involving bestiality and rape. Like Ford's, Hill's testimony inspired a generation of women and survivors. In her autobiography *Speaking Truth to Power*, she wrote: 'To my supporters I represent the courage to come forward and disclose a painful truth – a courage which thousands of others have found since the hearing.'[2]

But the comparison between Anita Hill and Christine Blasey Ford can only go so far. Hill, a Black woman, had a much frostier reception than Ford did: even the National Association for the Advancement of Colored People (NAACP) announced that it would oppose Thomas's nomination 'with regret' (Thomas is also Black).[3] Hill was questioned by a group consisting entirely of white men. In an interview at Stanford University eleven years later, she wondered how those men, and others, might have reacted if she had been 'white, blond-haired and blue-eyed'.[4] That question was at least partially answered by the reaction to Christine Blasey Ford. Even Donald Trump called Ford a 'fine woman' and 'very credible witness' (before mocking her at a rally in Mississippi).

Hill's experience reflects what Moya Bailey and Trudy call 'misogynoir'.[5] This is the blend of sexism and racism that shapes Black women's experiences and led Kimberlé Crenshaw to coin the term 'intersectionality'. The stereotype of the violent Black man, which means that men of colour are usually treated harshly, was weaponised in this case by Thomas. He famously called himself the victim of a 'high-tech lynching'. And in order to exonerate him, Hill was painted as a 'Jezebel' who had asked for what she got.

More than 1,600 Black women signed the Sisters Testify proclamation protesting the treatment of Hill. This was organised by African American Women in Defense of Ourselves, and printed as a full-page advertisement in the *New York Times* and elsewhere. Throughout US history, it said, Black women had been sexually stereotyped as 'immoral, insatiable, perverse; the initiators in all sexual contacts, abusive or otherwise'. These stereotypes – rooted in colonialism, in slavery, in segregation – created the idea that Black women could not be sexually assaulted.[6] 'As Anita Hill's experience demonstrates,' the proclamation said, 'Black women who speak of these matters are not likely to be believed.'

There is a gap of twenty-seven years between the allegations made by Professor Anita Hill and Dr Christine *neoliberalism*

Blasey Ford. This may also be a factor. Commenting on Ford's allegations in a speech to tech employees in Houston, Hill remarked that a generation of women had taken Gender Studies since her own testimony, and that there were also more female journalists and more women coming forward with stories of abuse.[7] Hill's own part in these cultural shifts should not be underestimated. Like many Black women before and after her, she played a pivotal role in putting a key feminist issue on the agenda.

## The war on women

In a *New York Times* article on Hill's Houston speech, Clifford Krauss remarked that Hill's and Ford's testimonies 'bookended' an era in which the public had 'increasingly come to grips with the issues of sexual harassment and assault'. The testimonies also mark early and late stages of neoliberal capitalism, with its production of huge inequalities and insecurities, including ones related to gender. Neoliberalism puts the needs of the market above all else. It also creates market solutions for social problems – and as public sectors have shrunk, women's private burdens have grown. As capitalism has spread to new territories, women have been exploited and dispossessed. As all this has happened and more, the rhetoric of 'development' and 'choice' has hidden gender and other inequalities.[8]

There are profound connections between capital accumulation and violence against women. As scholar

and activist Sylvia Federici writes, capitalist development began with a war on women: the European
witch-hunts of the sixteenth and seventeenth centuries, which destroyed the female subjects, practices and
knowledges (especially of abortion and female sexuality) standing in the way of capital.[9] These persecutions
helped get all women under male control, confining
many in the private sphere as unpaid agents of social
reproduction. Gender was embedded in the bourgeois
nuclear family unit (exemplified in the 'family wage'
paid to men in later versions of the capitalist system).[10]
Men were also allowed to punish women's refusal of
domestic work, protected by the right to privacy which
still enables domestic violence.

Federici also identifies a new war on women being
waged right now. This involves rising violence, femicide and attacks on reproductive rights, happening
especially in sub-Saharan Africa, Latin America and
Southeast Asia. Today, capitalism is not spread by
imperial armies but by the private armies and security guards of mining and petroleum companies,
sanctioned by bodies such as the UN and the World
Bank. And similar to the other forms of colonialism
that preceded it, this has also involved land grabs, the
destruction of traditional communities and relations,
and hyper-exploitation of women's bodies and labour.
Globalisation, Federici writes, 'is a process of political recolonization intended to give capital uncontested
control over the world's natural wealth and human
labor, and this cannot be achieved without attacking

17

*'capitalism of limit'*

women, who are directly responsible for the reproduction of their communities'.[11]

In India and other countries, women have been forced to give up subsistence production and assist their husbands' commodity production instead. Women labour in agricultural fields and maquiladoras/ sweatshops, which are often unregulated and in which sexual harassment and violence are rife. Or they find work as migrants in sectors with few rights and protections, such as domestic work or the sex industry. Underground economies intensify, together with strategies to combat organised crime (which, in turn, exacerbate poverty), putting women at risk. Women have been sexually violated, tortured and murdered by both 'narcos' and security forces in Mexico's war on drugs.

The war on women is also being waged in the neoliberal West. We are living in what, drawing on sociologist Gargi Bhattacharyya, I will describe as a *capitalism of limit*: the engines of accumulation are stuttering because of economic and ecological crisis.[12] As political scientist Nancy Fraser writes, this has also produced a crisis of social reproduction, as the state withdraws from welfare commitments and capitalism 'eats its own tail'.[13] And recession following the 2008 financial crisis has justified austerity policies to protect markets through further downsizing, removing or selling off social supports, which has widened gaps between rich and poor (as well as providing opportunities for the disaster capitalism that profits from economic crisis and shifts public goods into private hands). Women

*precarity*

and children have borne the brunt of cuts, which have also been especially vicious for elderly people and/or people with disabilities.

As their caring burdens have grown, women (especially women of colour) have been pushed out of shrinking and increasingly automated labour markets. Women are the majority of the global proletariat in precarious, informal and 'gig' economy jobs or state-sanctioned 'welfare to work' programmes, picked up and then put down as capitalism requires and then rejects them. And when inequalities increase, so do domestic and sexual violence. In crisis economies with few social supports, men vent their frustrations on the women in their families who are expected to provide care with almost no resources. Financial pressures stop women leaving abusive relationships. And services for women disappear: in the UK, austerity budgets have caused one in four women's refuges to lose all government funding.[14]

Economic, social and ecological crisis has also helped catalyse the global swing to the right, in which marginalised groups have been blamed for scarcity and other problems not of their making. In a capitalism of limit, there is an intensified focus on protecting the global 'haves' from the 'have nots'. As more privileged people feel the material and existential anxiety that has long been a fact of life for everyone else, Others are (re)defined as surplus to requirement or as threats. The 2016 Brexit referendum in the UK captured growing (or perhaps increasingly explicit) anti-immigrant

19

sentiment. Similar currents propelled Donald Trump into the US presidency later that same year. Proto-fascist leaders have been elected (or re-elected) in other countries including Hungary, India, the Philippines and Brazil. Far-right parties are making inroads in parliaments across Europe and overseas, often supported by 'dark money' from Russia and/or the US Christian right.[15]

Hoarding and defending resources means reasserting borders. It also means reasserting white supremacy, class privilege, 'abled' bodies, masculinity and binary gender. Women are women and men are men; Brexit means Brexit. Philosopher Maria Lugones writes that while colonial capitalism imposed the ideology of het-eropatriarchy, it invented the ideology of race to control land, production and behaviour.[16] Although notions of race have a longer history, colonialism systematically 'raced' populations so they could be hyper-exploited, and eventually discarded, by capitalist production. Populations were also systematically gendered to facil-itate this process: women were subordinated to men and made solely responsible for social reproduction, and there were attempts to eradicate Indigenous gen-ders that did not fit the Western binary.

Echoing the historical colonial project, contem-porary far-right politics blends racism with attacks on feminists and LGBT (especially trans) people. In 2018 the white supremacist Donald Trump declared his intention to 'legislate transgender out of exist-ence' through changing the Title IX amendment to the Higher Education Act to define gender as determined by biological sex, and biological sex as immutable and determined by genitalia at birth. Also in 2018 Jair Bolsonaro was elected the 38th president of Brazil. In early 2019 he signed an executive order opening up Indigenous reserves to mining. In 2015 he had said: 'The Indians do not speak our language, they do not have money, they do not have culture. They are native peoples. How did they manage to get 13 per cent of the national territory?'[17] Bolsonaro is also a misogynist and 'proud homophobe' who has said he would be 'incapable of loving' a gay son.

## The war on 'gender ideology'

Bolsonaro's election platform positioned him as a key player in the ongoing war on 'gender ideology' being fought across the religious and extreme right. This war started in the 1990s, declared by the Vatican when gender began to enter the lexicon of the United Nations and other global institutions. Its key tactics are opposing women's rights (including, centrally, abortion); defending heterosexuality and the nuclear family; and opposing the substitution of the biological language of 'sex' with the social and cultural term 'gender'.

In 2019 the Vatican published a document entitled 'Male and Female He Created Them', circulated to Catholic schools across the world. This aimed to counter ideas that denied 'the natural difference between a man and a woman', claiming that gender theory intended to create a 'cultural and ideological revolution'. The insinuations of communism here are not accidental. In ex-Soviet countries, 'gender ideology' is often compared to, or associated with, Stalinist indoctrination. Feminism and other progressive movements are also frequently called 'Stalinist' on the Western political right.

Schools and universities are central battlegrounds for the war against 'gender ideology'. Education is seen as the nerve centre for indoctrination into progressive politics and/or LGBT identities. Bolsonaro has backed the Schools Without Political Parties campaign, which aims to crack down on left-leaning views and the use of the terms 'gender' and 'sexual orientation' in classrooms. And university Gender Studies programmes, which are often female dominated, are imagined as gender ideology's headquarters. Religious and far-right politicians and groups have consistently attempted to discredit this academic field by suggesting that it is unscientific and that its scholars are agents of an agenda to destroy the nuclear family, heterosexuality and traditional gender roles (which we are).

In 2018 Hungary's proto-fascist government banned Gender Studies on the grounds that it was an 'ideology not a science'. 'People are born either male or female', said a spokesman, 'and we do not consider it acceptable for us to talk about socially constructed genders.' Alternative for Germany (AfD), the first far-right party to enter the German Bundestag since the Second World War, has pledged to discontinue all Gender Studies

Identity pols

funding, university appointments and research.[18] And Gender Studies is the canary in the coalmine. It is the first casualty of right-wing strategies to undermine all progressive politics and thought. In 2019 Bolsonaro announced plans to end government funding of philosophy and sociology degrees: these subjects tend to house gender scholars, but this was also a broadening of the offensive.

Gender Studies is seen as the apex of what is scornfully called 'identity politics', which acts as a cipher for the resentments of those who feel equality has gotten out of hand. From being a fairly neutral description of struggles around issues such as gender, class and race, 'identity politics' has become a pejorative. The term is now used on the right (and by some on the left) to connote politics focused on difference and division, and grounded in grievances and parochial concerns. Critiques of 'identity politics' also have more liberal formulations couched in defence of 'Enlightenment values' such as individualism and science, or 'free speech' and exchange of ideas.

In contrast to identity politics, the politics of white men is seen as representing universal, and reasonable, concerns. It is claimed that these concerns are ignored or dismissed by 'identity politics' ideologues who cannot cope with critical thought. On the right, a 'reasonable' idea could be that there are two immutable, biological sexes and that you cannot change from one to the other. Or that variations in IQ are at least partially attributable to race. Or that perhaps people *'precious snowflakes'*

with disabilities would prefer to be sterilised 'for their own good'. Defences of such ideas, and complaints that their proponents are being silenced, are now made from high-profile platforms and to growing audiences. This is a bait and switch by which beliefs that have been dominant for centuries are repackaged and return as the telling of radical new truths.

'Identity politics' ideologues (also known as feminists, anti-racists, LGBT and disability rights activists and others) insist that instead of having a 'civilised debate' about these ideas, we should call them the discredited and reactionary nonsense they are. Because of this, we are defined as censorious and oppressive. As the far-right outlet *Breitbart* proclaimed on Facebook during Trump's election campaign: 'Liberal students are precious snowflakes whose ideas must never be challenged. They must forever be coddled and their tender feelings protected, as they are social justice warriors in training whom you will continue funding with your tax dollars.'

In 2017 the *Telegraph* newspaper in the UK claimed that Cambridge University student Lola Olufemi had forced her university to 'drop white authors' from its syllabus. In fact, Olufemi had merely made recommendations for including more authors of colour. And despite there being very little evidence of speakers being 'no platformed' in UK universities, in 2017 the Conservative government suggested that universities might be fined for excluding people with 'controversial' views. This backlash against 'precious snowflakes' exposes a key foundation of the current rightward shift: from a position of privilege, equality can feel like oppression.

The rejection of 'identity politics' is also the *raison d'être* of the growing 'intellectual dark web' of scholars who see themselves as mavericks and truth-tellers. Many are based outside mainstream academia, although some have university posts. Perhaps the most famous member of this group is the Toronto 'professor against political correctness' Jordan Peterson, who rages against feminism and 'cultural Marxism'. Although Peterson describes himself as a 'classical liberal', he is celebrated by the 'alt' right. In 2019 he launched a subscription-only, 'anti-censorship' website called Thinkspot. For a fee, this platform promises its writers that only a successful legal action will lead to their content being removed. And who did Peterson invite to put this commitment to the test? The far-right YouTuber and Gamergater Carl Benjamin (also known as Sargon of Akkad).[19]

In 2017 three scholars associated with the intellectual dark web orchestrated a hoax against Gender Studies and other disciplines. This involved submitting 20 fake articles to academic journals in Gender, Queer, Masculinities, Fat and Sexuality Studies; Critical Race and Critical Whiteness Theory; Psychoanalysis; Sociology; and Educational Philosophy. The hoax was eventually exposed in 2018 when editors of one of the journals began to suspect that the paper submitted to them, and already published, was not genuine.

*the family*

The stated aim of the hoaxers was to expose the corruption of scholarship in what they called 'grievance studies'. Their demand was that universities undertake an immediate review of all the hoaxed areas of scholarship.[20]

## Weaponising 'women's safety'

Right-wing attacks on feminism and Gender Studies are a defence of the heterosexual nuclear family. This is also a defence of capital and nation: protecting 'our' economy and 'our' way of life. It is impossible to disentangle the war against 'gender ideology' from the widespread racism and anti-immigrant sentiment directed at other Others also seen as threats. 'Taking our country back' and 'making it great again' means closing our doors against, expelling or assimilating anyone who dares to produce, reproduce or think differently. It means reasserting geographical *and* ideological borders: defending the normatively gendered, cis, white, enabled and 'economically productive' capitalist body against those on the outside. It means emphasising reproductive (hetero)sex.

This structural violence is linked to an uptick in physical forms: as the far right go on the march, there has been an increase in racist, homophobic and transphobic attacks on the streets. And these can be fatal, especially to the most marginalised. In the US, Brazil and many other countries, there is a pattern of deadly violence against trans women of colour. There have also been a number of major anti-Black, Islamophobic, antisemitic and homophobic mass shootings in both the US and overseas. There is evidence that men who perpetrate mass shootings are often domestic abusers as well, reflecting how white supremacy and heteropatriarchy go hand-in-hand.[21]

There has also been an explosion of harassment online. Gamergate started in 2014 – this was a targeted harassment campaign against games developers Zoë Quinn and Brianna Wu, feminist journalist Anita Sarkeesian and a number of women in the video games industry, which quickly escalated to rape and death threats. Many Gamergaters resented what they saw as the increasing influence of feminism on gamer culture. Gamergate was not the first such campaign – but it took a developing culture war mainstream, became a recruiting ground for Trump supporters and created a blueprint for subsequent far-right actions. The home addresses of Sarkeesian, Quinn and Wu were all leaked, and all three were forced to flee. Sarkeesian also received a number of terrorist threats pertaining to public speaking engagements.

Online misogyny has also become (deadly) flesh in mass killings in the US and Canada perpetrated by 'incels' (involuntary celibates), who blame women for their lack of access to sex. In 2014 Elliot Rodger killed six people in Isla Vista, California, after emailing a 141-page autobiography to several people he knew. The document explored his mental health and frustration over his virginity, and called the killings 'manosphere'   Trump

a 'day of retribution'. Rodger was cited as an inspiration by Alex Minassian, another self-identified incel who drove his van into a crowd in Toronto in 2018, killing ten people and injuring a further sixteen. Both incels and Gamergaters are key factions in the online 'manosphere', a technological primordial soup for the gestation of far-right activists.[22]

Following Rodger's rampage Carl Benjamin blamed the deaths on feminism, calling it a 'disease of the modern age' that was now controlling society and had disenfranchised and radicalised young men. In the 2019 European elections, Benjamin stood as an MEP (Member of the European Parliament) candidate for the UK Independence Party (UKIP), which had been a central driver of Brexit. During his campaign, he defended a tweet he had sent previously to Labour MP Jess Phillips, which said he 'wouldn't even bother' to rape her. He was being accused of 'crimes against political correctness', he said. Phillips said she received 600 rape threats following Benjamin's tweet.[23]

Benjamin's comment to Phillips echoed one made by Bolsonaro in 2014, when during a parliamentary debate, he told MP Maria do Rosario she was 'too ugly' to rape. And across the world, reactionary politicians have expressed their privilege and entitlement via violence against women. Trump was elected president following multiple allegations: he has been publicly accused of sexual assault or misconduct by at least 22 women since the 1980s. He is the ultimate example of how economic and sexual predation go

Johusan

'Wolf Pack' Seville

hand-in-hand. Trump's campaign CEO Steve Bannon, former executive chairman of Breitbart News, has faced domestic violence charges. Polish right-winger Jaroslaw Iwaszkiewicz, a European Parliament ally of Brexit Party leader Nigel Farage, is reported to have said domestic violence 'would help bring many wives back down to earth'.[24]

A month before he assumed the UK premiership in 2019, police were called to the residence of Boris Johnson and his partner Carrie Symonds, following shouting and banging which got so loud that neighbours were concerned for Symonds's welfare. At one point she was heard telling Johnson to 'get off me'.[25] Johnson is notorious for his sexism, racism and homophobia. He has called Black people 'piccaninnies' and said that Muslim women wearing burqas look like letterboxes. He has called gay men 'tank-topped bumboys'. In 2007 he chose to endorse Hillary Clinton for the Democratic presidential nomination by saying she had 'dyed blonde hair and pouty lips, and a steely blue stare, like a sadistic nurse in a mental hospital'.[26]

The far right have also made political gains by opposing feminist movements against violence, exemplified by the 2016 'Wolf Pack' case in Spain. This involved a gang rape perpetrated against an 18-year-old woman at a festival in Seville. The charges were downgraded to sexual abuse when the verdict was released in 2018, which galvanised a wave of feminist resistance. And as women took to the streets, banging pots and pans, this in turn galvanised the far right. A counter-movement of men formed online, and the far-right party Vox gained supporters through tirades against 'radical feminism'. Later in 2018, Vox became the first far-right party to win multiple seats in Spain since the death of Franco.[27]

Like the generations of colonisers and 'founding fathers' before them, these men assert their right to 'take' and 'have' women while they grab, hoard and defend economic resources. But they also weaponise the idea of (white) 'women's safety' for the same political ends. As the Brexit referendum loomed, Farage claimed that women could be at risk of 'sex attacks' from gangs of migrant men if Britain remained in the European Union. In his presidential campaign, Trump made similar comments about Mexican men crossing the border. 'Women's safety' has also been central to debates about transgender equality, in which conservatives have situated trans women as potential rapists who want to invade 'women's space'.

In 2018 UKIP appointed far-right anti-Islam ideologue 'Tommy Robinson' (real name Stephen Yaxley-Lennon) as its advisor on 'grooming gangs'. A year later, Yaxley-Lennon was found in contempt of court for live-streaming film of defendants accused of sexually exploiting girls, in breach of a reporting ban and in interference with the course of justice. As the judgment was made, his supporters clashed with police and journalists outside the Old Bailey and chanted 'shame on you'.[28]

This concern with white 'women's safety' is not new; nor does it contradict the abuse perpetrated by powerful and privileged men. It reflects our status as property (and historically, we literally were): we are possessions of these men, to be used and abused but violently defended from the Others, especially when economic interests are at stake. The white and bourgeois rape victim has been a key motif in colonial expansion, as well as 'law and order' and anti-immigration agendas in richer countries which protect the 'haves' from the 'have nots'. Sometimes, sexual violence is a 'cultural problem' (but only when this culture is non-white). Sometimes, it is a product of male anatomy (but only when this anatomy is assigned to a trans woman or a man of colour). Sexual violence is never the violence of heteropatriarchy or globalising racial capital. Instead, representatives of patriarchy, capitalism and colonialism weaponise the idea of 'women's safety' against marginalised and hyper-exploited groups.

## The intersectionality of struggles

The Kavanaugh hearings exemplified the misogyny and violent entitlement of an administration headed by its own 'predator-in-chief'. But support for Dr Ford was bolstered by a growing resistance. The resurgent right has been met by a younger, more diverse and more radical international left, which is beginning to achieve electoral success. The movement around Jeremy Corbyn, which produced a hung parliament in the 2017 UK general election, is one example. In the

2019 European elections, while far-right parties did well, so did progressive ones: green parties especially won a significant proportion of the vote.

The US midterms in 2018 saw record wins for women of colour. These included Sharice Davids and Deb Haaland, the first Native American women elected to Congress. They also included the four women now known as 'The Squad': Ayanna Pressley, the first Black woman elected to Congress from Massachusetts, Ilhan Omar and Rashida Tlaib, the first Muslim congress-women, and Alexandria Ocasio-Cortez. Since being elected, these women have collectively pushed progressive policies. They have also called out Trump's racism, at great political and personal risk.

With Trump's sexual transgressions still prominent in the public imagination, women's success in the 2018 midterms was partly put down to #MeToo. And #MeToo is part of a worldwide feminist resurgence, in the mainstream and outside it. The hashtag trended in at least 85 countries, with 1.7 million tweets and 12 million Facebook posts in the first six weeks.[29] There were allied hashtags such as #YoTambien in Spain and Latin America, #BalanceTonPorc (expose your pig) in France, and #RiceBunny in China where the original hashtag faced censorship. Google's repository #MeToo Rising contains information on many initiatives inspired by the movement, in countries across the world. For instance, in India it caused a renewal of mainstream concern with sexual violence not seen since the gang rape and murder of Jyoti Singh Pandey in 2012.[30] #MeToo also rejuvenated many pre-existing sexual violence projects in universities, in political institutions and in radical communities.

#MeToo reshaped – and continues to reshape – public understandings of sexual violence. At its best, it linked sexual violence with the 'everyman' rather than the 'bad man' through the volume of personal stories shared. It showed how frequently harassment and assault are perpetrated and normalised. It put all men on the spot, asking them to reflect on their own behaviour and their role in that of others. And it led to various legal reforms: for instance, a 2019 study by the US National Women's Law Center found that following #MeToo, fifteen states passed laws protecting employees from gender discrimination and sexual harassment at work.[31]

But the position of #MeToo and mainstream feminism in the contemporary political field is complex. This is because narratives about gender and intersecting inequalities are being rejuvenated, fought *and weaponised*. There is a war on women raging worldwide, and an answering feminist resurgence. There is an ongoing backlash against progressive movements, which incorporates attacks on 'gender ideology', feminism and 'identity politics', and reasserts privilege in economic crisis. And 'protecting women' is being kicked around as a political football in the context of expanding authoritarian governments and states, and more open racism and bigotry. This is a very difficult field to navigate.

And this raises questions that are persistent and urgent, if not new, about the role of contemporary activism against sexual violence. On this political terrain, it is more important than ever to consider what activist and scholar Angela Davis calls the 'intersectionality of struggles'.[32] How might mainstream feminist activism help or hinder other social justice projects, for instance around class inequality, race discrimination, migrants' rights and transgender inclusion? When violent men and governments profess their concern for 'women's safety', how should feminists respond? Do the ends always justify the means? These questions are particularly pressing for movements such as #MeToo, which gain power through providing clickbait for the 'outrage economy' of the corporate media. They are also particularly pressing for mainstream feminism because it is dominated by white and privileged women.

## 2

# Me, not you

In 2006 Black feminist Tarana Burke created an organisation to help survivors of sexual violence, particularly young women of colour, find pathways to healing. Reflecting her central principle of empowerment through empathy, Burke named her programme of work 'Me Too'. In 2017 the phrase went viral as a hashtag, following allegations against film producer Harvey Weinstein by a number of famous women in Hollywood. 'If you've been sexually harassed or assaulted,' tweeted Alyssa Milano, 'write "me too" as a reply to this tweet.' #MeToo is arguably one of the biggest media and cultural moments in recent Western history, focused on sexual violence.

A study by the Pew Research Center a year after Milano's intervention estimated that 19 million tweets had used the hashtag: more than 55,000 tweets per day.[1] Analysis of over 600,000 Twitter and Facebook posts tagged with #MeToo showed that they varied: some shared personal stories, some re-posted articles, some expressed general support or offered commentary, and some discussed offenders.[2] However, perhaps because of the declarative nature of the hashtag and the testimonial media cultures it was shared in, #MeToo was generally viewed as a mass disclosure.

'Speaking out' is central to feminist politics,[3] from Sojourner Truth's speech to the 1851 Akron Women's Rights Convention, to the testimonial activism of Black women in the US Civil Rights movement, to the phrase 'the personal is political' which illuminated the consciousness-raising sessions of Women's Liberation. Sexism produces silence, so speech has been associated with breaking free; sharing experiences of oppression can foster understanding and resistance. In her story of recovery from breast cancer, poet and writer Audre Lorde asked: 'What are the words you do not yet have? What do you need to say? What are the tyrannies you swallow day by day and attempt to make your own, until you will sicken and die of them, still in silence?'[4]

Lorde's words express the belief that putting our trauma 'out there' is a way to escape being consumed by it 'in here'. This is especially the case with sexual violence. For survivors, speaking out can legitimise feelings of violation and stop us blaming ourselves. We can reclaim subjectivity and control after they have been taken away. Speaking out is also a way to raise awareness – the personal is political, after all. The personal is also, increasingly, economic: trauma narratives are investment capital in the media 'outrage economy'. But some stories are worth more than others.

Soon after Milano's tweet a group of Black women, including author Luvvie Ajayi and TV presenter Bevy

*Interrupting*

Smith, called for her to acknowledge Tarana Burke as the founder of #MeToo. To her credit, she did – and the two became known as the movement's leaders. In December 2017 they were jointly interviewed on the US *Today* show. But Milano was criticised for speaking over Burke, interrupting her answers to questions and taking up most of the airtime. This interview functions as a metaphor for the mainstream feminist movement against sexual violence. 'Speaking out' can become 'speaking over' a lot of the time. This is not 'Me, Too' – it is more like 'Me, Not You'.

## 'Feminism' is for white women

The #MeToo hashtag had global reach. But except for Burke, most key figures in the movement were Western, white and privileged. As Black actor and sexual violence activist Gabrielle Union said on *Good Morning America*, 'I think the floodgates have opened for white women.' The whiteness of #MeToo reflects two related issues: the global ascendancy of mainstream Western feminism (which sees itself as universal and neutral), and the dominance of white bourgeois women within it.

As #MeToo played out in the mainstream media, it often appeared to be a conversation between white people: the privileged white women speaking out and the privileged white men defending themselves against allegations. Interjections were also made by the white men – *and women* – who led the backlash. Social media narratives were more diverse, reflecting the fact that social media can be a more democratic space. But even on social media, privileged white people's voices tend to be the ones rising above the cacophony. Access to, and success on, social media platforms is driven by time and resources (especially for people in lower-income countries). And there are very clear ideas about whose voices count.[5]

#MeToo is the latest in a long list of feminist movements in which white bourgeois women have co-opted the ideas and resistance of women of colour. Second-wave white feminists drew on the anti-rape activism of Black women in the US Civil Rights movement, but did not give them any credit. (In fact, Susan Brownmiller claimed in 1975 that anti-rape organising was an *invention* of Women's Liberation.)[6] Activism by women of colour (and Professor Anita Hill in particular) has been crucial to fighting workplace sexual harassment, but white academics and lawyers have tended to receive the acclaim.

And while the work of women of colour is co-opted, white feminist outrage has overlooked them. #MeToo was no different in this regard: commentators noted a focus on privileged white women in the West, rather than the Black girls abused by R. Kelly or the Rohingya women raped in Myanmar. There was also little connection between #MeToo and coexisting actions focused on the intersections between gender and race – for instance, the Predatory Peacekeepers campaign started by Samantha Asumadu and Guilaine Kinouani in 2016, which brought attention to violence committed by UN peacekeepers against girls and women in African countries, or Ni Una Menos (not one less), which originated in Argentina and spread across Latin America. Under its banner, protestors have taken to the streets over femicide or 'feminicidio', meaning violence against people who are feminised or regarded as feminine.

The hashtag #SolidarityIsForWhiteWomen, created by author Mikki Kendall in 2013, has become a marker of these dynamics. And it is poignant that when #MeToo started trending, #SolidarityIsForWhiteWomen did as well. This was in response to #WomenBoycottTwitter, an action called after one of Weinstein's accusers, actor Rose McGowan, was suspended from the platform. Black feminists used #SolidarityIsForWhiteWomen to point out that boycotts had not been called over the persistent harassment of many Black women. They named actor Leslie Jones, subjected to a campaign of racist and misogynist abuse from Gamergater and 'alt'-right troll Milo Yiannopoulous and his followers, over her role in the all-female *Ghostbusters* reboot the previous year.

#SolidarityIsForWhiteWomen was originally created to highlight the support given by prominent white feminists to Gender Studies professor Hugo Schwyzer. Schwyzer had built his platform largely by defending white feminists and attacking feminists of colour.[7] And the solidarities between white women and white men, even in the face of allegations of violence, may

be the Achilles heel of the mainstream feminist movement. During #MeToo, actor, writer and director Lena
Dunham was widely criticised for her defence of *Girls*
writer Murray Miller, accused of rape by actor Aurora
Perrineau. Dunham later apologised and admitted
that she had lied about the extent of her knowledge
of the incident.[8] (UK Labour MP Jess Phillips supported Dunham, in an article in the *Guardian* entitled 'Abusive men are everywhere – and some of us
love them'.)[9]

Alyssa Milano was also criticised after defending the
'warm, generous' former vice president Joe Biden, following allegations of inappropriate touching by former
Democratic Nevada state representative Lucy Flores
and former congressional aide Amy Lappos. These
allegations also prompted discussion of Biden's role
as chair of the Senate Judiciary Committee which
had confirmed Clarence Thomas's nomination to the
Supreme Court. Biden, it was reported, had refused to
allow testimony from witnesses who could have cor-
roborated Anita Hill's allegations, and sat back while
Republicans on the committee attacked her. As Aimee
Allison wrote in *The Nation*, 'his disrespect of Hill
inflicted deep pain on women of color at the time'.[10]
The fact that Milano saw him as an ally speaks vol-
umes about white feminism.

## Sexual violence in white feminism

Mainstream Western feminism has always been marked by exclusion. First-wave women's suffrage campaigners Elizabeth Cady Stanton and Susan B. Anthony advocated the abolition of slavery, but opposed the 15th Amendment that in 1870 secured voting rights for men of any race but not for women. 'I will cut off this right arm of mine before I will ask for the ballot for the Negro and not for the woman', Anthony said in 1866. The previous year, Cady Stanton had written: 'it becomes a serious question whether we had better stand aside and see "Sambo" walk into the kingdom first'.[11]

In Britain, suffragist Millicent Fawcett was similarly outraged that while her countrywomen lacked the vote, Maori women in 'the colonies' did not. (In 2018, a statue of Fawcett was erected in Parliament Square following a campaign by white feminists.) And Emmeline Pankhurst's famous quote 'I'd rather be a rebel than a slave' exemplified the way that privileged women in the movement co-opted – and downplayed – racist oppression. This manoeuvre dates back at least to Mary Wollstonecraft's 1792 text *A Vindication of the Rights of Woman* (although Wollstonecraft was an abolitionist, she frequently compared women to 'slaves'). It also continues to be executed by white bourgeois feminists. In 2015 actors Carey Mulligan, Meryl Streep, Anne-Marie Duff and Romola Garai – all starring in the film *Suffragette* – were photographed in T-shirts sporting

Pankhurst's quote.[12] In 2017 Rose McGowan posted, and then deleted, a tweet comparing the word 'women' with 'the n word'.[13]

While first-wave white feminism was concerned with women's suffrage, health and education, the second wave that swelled in the 1960s focused on knottier problems such as sexuality, abortion and rape. 'The personal is political' was the rallying cry. Mainstream feminist ideas about sexual violence date mainly from this time and reflect the domination of activism and scholarship by bourgeois white women. Although the literature is not homogeneous, the best-known texts tend to have a one-dimensional focus on gender. The 'woman question', in Catharine MacKinnon's words, was *the* question,[14] and many radical feminists in particular saw women as a 'sex class' defined by their capacity to reproduce. In her 1970 book *The Dialectic of Sex*, Shulamith Firestone wrote: 'unlike economic class, sex class sprang directly from a biological reality: men and women were created different, and not equal'.[15] For Firestone and others, this 'natural reproductive difference' was the first division of labour.

War between the 'sex classes' was theorised as the cause of sexual violence. In *Against Our Will*, perhaps the most famous feminist book on rape, Susan Brownmiller argued that it was not an act of uncontrolled desire but 'a conscious process of intimidation by which *all men* keep *all women* in a state of fear'. Both acts and threats of sexual violence maintained patriarchal power. Susan Griffin decried the 'patriarchal protection racket': the threat of stranger rape that made women look for protection from their male partners and family members, who were actually more likely to abuse them.[16] Liz Kelly placed rape on a continuum of acts, from sexual harassment to sexualised murder, which all functioned to keep women under control.[17] Prostitution and other forms of sex work were also seen as sexual violence, 'paid rape' that expressed and legitimated male sexual entitlement (or in socialist and Marxist feminism, as forms of sexual appropriation that derived from the appropriation of women's reproductive labour in capitalist society).

The structural interpretation of rape as terrorism led to important legal changes, as sexual violence was reinterpreted as *violence*. This helped reframe rape as a crime instead of 'sex gone wrong'. It helped position it as a violation rather than a man's (especially a husband's) right. It helped prohibit the use of sexual history evidence in court (although in practice this continued to happen). The idea of rape as terrorism also echoed, without credit, the Black feminist politics of the Civil Rights movement and earlier. But there were important differences: second-wave white feminists writing about rape rarely engaged with the intersections between gender, class and race (the work of Marxist feminist Maria Mies is a notable exception). If they had, their understandings of sexual violence would have needed to account for how *allegations* could also be used to justify economic exploitation and white supremacy.

Instead, second-wave white feminists focused on the war on women – and its key weapon was the penis. Brownmiller mused that man's discovery of his genitalia 'as a weapon to generate fear' ranked alongside the discovery of fire or the making of the 'first crude stone axe'.[18] Other feminists used the metaphor of the penis as invader, appropriating the language of anti-colonial struggles. For Kate Millett, male dominance was 'interior colonisation'.[19] In *Intercourse*, Andrea Dworkin wrote:

> There is no analogue anywhere among subordinated groups of people to this experience of being made for intercourse: for penetration, entry, occupation. There is no analogue in occupied countries or in dominated races or in imprisoned dissidents or in colonialized cultures or in the submission of children to adults or in the atrocities that have marked the twentieth century ranging from Auschwitz to the Gulag.[20]

This quote exemplifies second-wave radical feminism in its description of women as a sex class that is uniquely and maximally oppressed. And it exemplifies how this dismissed or even erased the racist oppression of people of colour. Violence was located in the male body, while women were the violated ones – this hid the victimisation of men of colour, which has often been sexual and sometimes perpetrated by white women (a recent example is the sexual torture of prisoners in Abu Ghraib). The idea that women could perpetrate violence was largely discounted in radical feminism. So was the fact that for some women, other biological markers could evoke equal or even greater threats than the penis: for instance, white skin.[21]

The view of the penis as weapon and/or invader also meant that for some radical feminists, the act of (hetero)sex itself was not that different from rape. For Millett, coitus was a 'model of sexual politics on an individual or personal plane'.[22] It was an eroticised performance of dominance and submission. And for MacKinnon this made women's consent meaningless, because they had been socialised to acquiesce. This critique of femininity and how consent functions in conditions of inequality was important: it helped create understanding of why many women did not fight back against assaults. It challenged prevailing myths that defined a 'real rape' as one in which there was evidence of a struggle.

But the submissive femininity of radical feminism was bourgeois, white and heterosexual. There was no acknowledgement that this 'enslaved' femininity was not universal, or that it was complicit in the *actual enslavement* of generations of Black people. Germaine Greer's 'female eunuch' – a castrated, impotent being praised for her timidity and delicacy – may have been downtrodden at home, but outside it she was an emblem of capitalist and colonial exploitation.[23] While white bourgeois men dominated their wives, they also used 'respectable' femininity to define women of colour and working-class white women as inferior.[24] And when bourgeois white women were raped by men who were not their husbands, there was outrage (and violent retribution). Meanwhile, women of colour (Black women especially) and white women of the labouring social classes were usually blamed for their own victimisation (and continue to be).

## Carceral feminism, colonial feminism

First- and second-wave white feminism had two major outgrowths – carceral feminism and colonial feminism, which are inextricably linked. While modern states were founded on genocide and slavery, colonial violence shaped 'law and order' agendas in domestic contexts too. Carceral feminism, as defined by sociologist Elizabeth Bernstein, sees criminalisation and incarceration as ways to achieve gender justice. It focuses especially on sexual violence, as well as prostitution and trafficking (which are seen as forms of sexual violence). It can have conservative and liberal guises: some feminists have embraced ideas of 'fighting crime', 'naming and shaming', 'family values' and 'building democracy overseas', while others have entered into unwitting alliances with conservatives under the rubric of 'rescuing women'.[25]

Carceral feminism pays little or no attention to the people of colour and working-class white people who tend to be the targets of punitive state systems and community retribution. Baroness Valerie Amos and writer/film-maker Pratibha Parmar have highlighted how white feminists often remain silent when the media provoke outrage about 'Black rapists' and 'white victims'. Carceral feminists have also played into the hands of right-wing vigilantes: Amos and Parmar describe how 'Reclaim the Night' marches through Black inner-city areas have intersected with state policing of the streets, and inspired groups wanting to protect white women by beating up Black men.[26]

For carceral feminists, sexual violence, prostitution and trafficking are the fault of 'bad men' (often implicitly men of colour) who need to be punished. The power relations of patriarchal capitalism, the austerity regimes that push poor women into selling sex and stop them leaving abusive relationships, and the border regimes that make migrant women dependent on traffickers do not enter this analysis. The 'bad men' are also usually strangers, despite the history of other feminists insisting that the family is most often the site of abuse.

Carceral feminism is the vengeful sister of what Janet Halley and her co-authors call 'governance feminism', in which feminist activists and community support networks have found more formal roles within the state.[27] It is influenced by the general shift from the welfare to the carceral state in attempts to tackle inequality (or more precisely, its effects). Political scientist Kristin Bumiller writes that, in the 1990s, a myopic feminist focus on the criminalisation of violence against women outstripped concerns about structural gender oppression.[28] And as Bernstein argues, this neoliberal paradigm of 'feminism as crime control' was then spread across the globe.

47

This exporting of Western feminist principles has a long history and completes the circuit between carceral and colonial feminism. Divinity scholar Leila Ahmed defines colonial feminism as feminism 'used against other cultures' in the service of oppression, exploitation and genocide.[29] Connecting 'culture' and the status of women was a key colonial manoeuvre. It implied that progress could only be achieved by abandoning Indigenous ways of life and embracing the ways of the invaders. In late nineteenth- and early twentieth-century Egypt, a concern with veiling was often professed by British men (who did not support women's suffrage back home). In South Asia there were campaigns against sati, child marriage and other practices. Feminist theorist Gayatri Spivak calls this 'civilising' mission 'white men saving brown women from brown men'.[30] White women were also heavily involved, from the philanthropists and Christian missionaries who devoted their lives to 'saving' their Muslim sisters, to the anthropologists who studied Indigenous communities.

And women's oppression overseas continues to be repackaged as an effect of 'culture', not of colonialism itself. The neo-colonial War on Terror was justified in terms of liberating women from 'barbaric regimes', a narrative pushed in speeches by 'first ladies' Laura Bush and Cherie Blair, who enlisted women to justify intervention.[31] The Bush administration fostered a conservative/feminist alliance, and various feminist individuals and organisations publicly embraced its anti-trafficking initiatives and military intervention in Afghanistan and Iraq.[32] In these contemporary versions of colonial feminism, Other women need to be schooled in the feminist ideas of the West. White feminists are 'saving' Black and brown women by encouraging them to be more like us.

As anthropologist Lila Abu-Lughod points out, the feminist mission to rescue women from the Taliban did not also call for a global redistribution of wealth.[33] Colonial feminists are concerned with 'liberating' Other women, not critiquing colonial capitalism and its neoliberal successor. Colonial feminists condemn the burqa, but not the wars waged or fought by proxy in the service of resource accumulation, trade routes and pipelines, enabling and supporting autocratic and fundamentalist regimes. Their main focus is not the deliberately uneven development that impoverishes some countries and enriches others, creating a global societal division of labour as well as massive domestic inequalities. With its fixation on gender, white feminism has little capacity to understand these intersecting dynamics. This differentiates it dramatically from Black feminism and other feminisms of colour.

## A different tradition

In her famous article 'Mapping the Margins', law scholar Kimberlé Crenshaw explained the idea of intersectionality through a critique of white feminist initiatives around violence against women. She argued that issues faced by Black women existed on three levels.

They were structural: factors such as poverty or language barriers, which made it difficult for women of
colour to access women's services. They were political:
violence against Black women fell through the cracks
between white feminism (which did not want violence
sidelined as a 'minority issue') and Black anti-racism
(which rejected stereotypes of Black men as violent).
And they were representational: the construction of
Black men as uniquely violent had its mate in the idea
of Black women as always up for sex (and therefore,
impossible to rape).[34]

For Crenshaw, these issues reflected the intersections
between race and gender (and other categories such as
class and sexuality). This meant that Black women's
experiences could not be fully understood by one-
dimensional frameworks. It also meant that sexism and
racism in general were poorly understood, as politics and
theories did not account for the experiences of the most
marginalised. Focusing on gender *or* race can only benefit
white women who are not oppressed by race or Black men
who are not oppressed by gender. Intersectionality, in
contrast, sees oppressions as co-constituted and simultaneous, rather than separate and different. It is about
how the intersecting structures of heteropatriarchy,
racial capitalism and colonialism make certain identity
categories more vulnerable than others.

Although Crenshaw is widely credited with
popularising the term, intersectionality grew out of
a long tradition of Black women's resistance against
interlocking oppressions. Sojourner Truth's speech to

the Akron Women's Convention emphasised both her Blackness and her womanhood, later immortalised in the famous question: 'Ain't I a Woman?' Harriet Jacobs's 1861 emancipation narrative documented the racist brutalisation of enslaved women through rape, forced pregnancy and separation from their children. Because of its regularity in the lives of colonised and enslaved people, from the outset Black feminism and womanism has centred sexual violence.

But Black feminism has taken a multidimensional approach to sexual violence, because of how *allegations* of rape have been used as tools of white supremacy. Ida B. Wells, a pivotal figure in the anti-lynching movement, showed that in many cases allegations were false or there had been consensual relations between white women and Black men. Wells saw lynching not as vigilante justice but as a racist technology of terror. Mary Church Terrell and other activists similarly argued that allegations of rape were a justification for lynching and often nothing more.[35]

The Civil Rights movement included many sexual violence activists, including Rosa Parks. Their work fed the Black women's organisations of the 1960s and 1970s, which critiqued the white mainstream and (more importantly) inscribed their own theories and practised their own politics. In 1968 women from the US Student Non-Violent Coordinating Committee set up the Third World Women's Alliance, bringing together Black, Asian and Latinx feminists and others. In 1973 a group of Black feminists, including Florynce

Kennedy, Alice Walker and Barbara Smith, formed the National Black Feminist Organization (NBFO). A year later, Smith joined a group of other Black lesbian feminists to found the Boston-based Combahee River Collective, a self-consciously radical alternative to the NBFO.

All these groups focused on challenging intersecting oppressions – race, gender, heterosexuality and class – and developing integrated analysis and action. Combahee and the Third World Women's Alliance were socialist and anti-imperialist, addressing the links between identity-based oppression and capitalist exploitation. And in contrast to the radical feminism which emerged in the 1960s, Black feminism was not a separatist movement. Black feminists had solidarity with Black men around racism, and aimed to build coalitions with anti-racist white women and gender-progressive Black men.

Reflecting these multiple solidarities, Black feminist scholarship on rape was complex. As Angela Davis wrote in 1985:

> Rape bears a direct relationship to all of the existing power structures in a given society ... [and if] we do not attempt to understand the nature of sexual violence as it relates to racial, class, and governmental violence and power, we can not even begin to develop strategies which will allow us to eventually purge our society of the oppressiveness of rape.[36]

In her book *Women, Race and Class*, Davis related rape to misogyny, domestic racism and global capitalist imperialism. She explored how colonial ideas of Black sexual 'savagery' created the notions of the Black man as rapist and the Black woman as un-rapeable (as Saidiya Hartman writes, this also framed a persistent association of Black women with prostitution).[37] Along with other Black feminist scholars, Davis also argued that the carceral systems favoured by white feminists were grounded in, and perpetuated, racist and classist violence.

Black feminists worked alongside other women of colour who had similarly rich, multidimensional politics.[38] For instance, Chicana feminists, First Nations and Native American feminists and feminists of the South Asian diaspora combined gender analysis with analysis of colonial violence and genocide. They documented how the bodies of Indigenous people were both sexually violated by colonisers and seen as 'polluted' with sexual sin (which also justified mass sterilisation and other abuses). They argued that while white women were bearers of the imperial order, Indigenous women were seen as bearers of the counter-imperial order, which justified their rape and murder and the murder of their children.[39] They exposed how Indigenous men and people who did not conform to bourgeois binary gender (for instance, hijras in South Asia and people who are now called Two Spirit in Native American cultures) were also sexually humiliated, victimised, mutilated and killed. For these feminists, the fight against colonialism could not be separated from the fight against sexual violence.

Sexual violence was also seen as a product of dysfunctional capitalist societies, and although there were
concerns about romanticising Indigenous cultures, they
were generally interpreted as more peaceful and not so
rigidly gendered. Capitalism drove the 'rape' of colonised land, seen as 'raw material' of which Indigenous
people were an unwanted part. The Western history of
sexual violence is also capitalism's history: it is linked
to women's historical status as property and ongoing status as reproducers of nation and life. It is also
a device of the hierarchical and adversarial relations
which characterise the greedy market economy. In
contrast to conquering soldiers (and in stark contrast
to their depiction in both historical and contemporary
popular culture), Native American warriors who captured European women did not tend to victimise them.
Between 1675 and 1763, almost 40 per cent of white
women taken captive by Native American people in
New England chose to remain with their captors.[40]

Feminists of colour and post-colonial feminists continue to highlight, and resist, the way violence is used
against Indigenous communities who get in the way of
capitalist expansion. As Gargi Bhattacharyya argues,
the colonial idea of expendable populations and regions
is key to contemporary economic models.[41] Indigenous
lands are violently appropriated as 'sacrifice zones'
for the dumping of toxic waste, the location of power
plants or fracking, which affects people's bodies and
reproductive systems. And the 'man camps' set up
for workers in the oil pipeline, mining, hydroelectric

and forestry industries have been associated with an increase in rape.[42]

A 2010 US Department of Justice report found that 56 per cent of Native American women had experienced sexual violence, the majority perpetrated by a non-Native American man (in comparison to other populations where perpetration by a man of the same racialised grouping is much more likely).[43] Sexual violence also continues to be central to conflicts worldwide, many of these driven by economic exploitation and resource extraction. Sexual violence is used against people of all genders by state and non-state actors, as a strategy of repression, terror and control. It is a tool of ethnic dilution through forced pregnancy. Colonialism is not over.

Feminists of colour, most of them members of the global proletariat, were behind various interventions into the Anglo-American mainstream of #MeToo that had a more intersectional and decolonial focus.[44] The Alianza Nacional de Campesinas, and similar groups of domestic workers and female janitors, highlighted abuse in their industries. McDonalds workers in ten US cities organised a day-long strike protesting sexual harassment. Hotel workers took to the streets in their thousands, and won their demand for panic buttons from five major chains. Members of the Coalition of Immokalee Workers conducted a week-long fast to demand that fast food giant Wendy's sign up to the Fair Food Program, which includes provisions to prevent and deal with sexual harassment. These actions were as much part of #MeToo as those of Alyssa Milano and other white feminists. However, they did not get nearly as much coverage. As I will argue in the next chapter and reflecting the history of white feminism, #MeToo was often 'Me, Not You'.

## Chapter 3

# Political whiteness

As #MeToo unfolded, perhaps second only to Harvey Weinstein in its cast of antagonists was gymnastics coach Larry Nassar.[1] In what is now called the 'USA gymnastics sex abuse scandal', Nassar was accused of molesting at least 250 girls and young women and one young man, between 1992 and 2016. In 2017 Nassar was sentenced to 60 years in federal prison after pleading guilty to child pornography charges. On 24 January 2018 he was sentenced to 40 to 175 years in a Michigan state prison after pleading guilty to seven counts of sexual assault of minors. On 5 February that year he was sentenced to an additional 40 to 125 years in prison after pleading guilty to a further three counts of sexual assault. Judge Rosemarie Aquilina, handing Nassar his second sentence, told him that, if authorised, she would have 'allow[ed] some or many people to do to him what he did to others'. 'I just signed your death warrant', she said.

A subsequent article in *Bustle* magazine, entitled 'Tweets about Judge Aquilina will make you fangirl so hard', described her as 'a bona-fide feminist icon'. It reported that women across the nation had praised her handling of the case, calling her 'queen of the courtroom', '#MeToo hero of the week' and advocating for new judicial awards to be created in her honour. A similarly celebratory article in *The Atlantic* was headlined the 'Transformative Justice of Judge Aquilina'.

Menominee feminist Kelly Hayes and Black feminist Mariame Kaba, writing in *The Appeal*, profoundly disagreed. Even when criminal punishment is handed down to a non-Black person, they wrote, it 'remains a structurally anti-Black apparatus, firmly rooted in the United States' ongoing reliance on the financial exploitation and social control of Black people'.[2] The signing of Nassar's 'death warrant', for them, was not transformative justice.

I am going to state the obvious: the bourgeois whiteness of mainstream feminism shapes what feminist theorist Clare Hemmings might call its political 'grammar'.[3] What Hemmings means by this is the form in which the movement's stories are told, and the assumptions and meanings these draw upon and create. There are several familiar narratives: for instance, that rape is perpetrated by 'bad men' who need to be exposed; that police exist to catch these men, and courts to judge them; that they ought to be punished severely for what they have done. Underneath these stories lie deeply held beliefs: people are either victims or perpetrators, but not both; the state is protective rather than oppressive; shaming and punishment work.

This grammar is what I call political whiteness. The term is not new: it has been used before, perhaps most prominently by Daniel Martinez HoSang in his book *Racial Propositions* (2010).[4] This analyses the politics of California, a state with a liberal political culture and increasingly diverse population, as it banned public services for undocumented immigrants, repealed affirmative action programmes, and outlawed bilingual education from the 1990s onwards. HoSang uses 'political whiteness' to describe the 'colour-blind' but implicitly ethno-nationalist politics that underpinned these initiatives, focused on 'our' rights, 'our' jobs, 'our' homes, 'our' kids and 'our' streets. I want to use the term differently. For me, political whiteness goes beyond the implicitly or explicitly 'whites first' orientation that is present in almost any politics dominated by white people. It has a complex inner landscape.

My analysis of political whiteness combines a critique of white feminism with reflections on how it is related to the backlash. As Sarah Banet-Weiser argues, 'popular misogyny' often turns popular feminism back on itself.[5] But these opposing movements also share profound emotional attachments: to the self (and often the wounded self) and to power (often in the form of the state). This produces a number of common characteristics: narcissism, alertness to threat (which in white women's case is almost always sexualised) and an accompanying need for control. It might seem insensitive to associate feminism with the misogynist backlash (or whitelash) against it. But acknowledging the central role of race demands that we do just that. And in a world moving rapidly to the right, in which white supremacy is being reasserted, it is crucial to interrogate the reactionary tendencies of white feminism (not that it wasn't before).

The idea of political whiteness begins from the premise that white subjectivities are shaped by the structural position of white supremacy, and that whiteness and class privilege are fractured, but not erased, by gender and other social relations. In other words, being a victim of gender violence does not absolve me of being a perpetrator of white supremacy and capitalist exploitation. A key principle of political whiteness, then, is that supremacy and victimhood are not mutually exclusive. Instead, the concept explores how they are – intimately – related.

You do not have to be white to engage in political whiteness. Some of the themes in this chapter pertain to Western politicians of colour and non-Western bourgeoisies as well. Black Lives Matter arose during the Obama administration, and African Americans critiqued Obama for many things, including his rhetoric around 'meritocracy' and escalation of the Afghanistan war. US Senator Kamala Harris has been challenged by Black feminists over her investment in the criminal punishment system, and so has Lori Lightfoot, the first openly lesbian and Black mayor of Chicago. When Boris Johnson became UK Prime Minister in 2019, he appointed four people of colour as cabinet ministers: Priti Patel, Sajid Javid, James Cleverly and Alok Sharma.

Black Studies Professor Kehinde Andrews described the four as 'some of the most rightwing figures even in the Tory party'.[6] When people from marginalised groups achieve success within racial capitalism, they often embody its values. But political whiteness tends to be *baked in* to the politics of white people, unless we actively try to sift it out. All white people do it at least some of the time. I have yet to meet one who doesn't, including myself.

## 'I'm everything' – narcissism in political whiteness

On International Women's Day 2019, Alyssa Milano tweeted: 'My transgender sisters! I am celebrating YOU this #NationalWomensDay!' Soon afterwards, a male user asked: 'Alyssa are you transgender?' Her response is worth repeating in full.

> I'm trans. I'm a person of color. I'm an immigrant. I'm a lesbian. I'm a gay man. I'm the disabled.
>
> I'm everything. And so are you, Kirk.
>
> Don't be afraid of what you don't know or understand. No one wants to hurt you. We are all just looking for our happily ever after.

Milano quickly followed this tweet with another one quoting thirteenth-century Persian poet and scholar Rumi: 'This is a subtle truth. Whatever you love, you are.'

This brief event can tell us much about white feminism. It is nominally inclusive, but inclusion is dependent on white women being centred as those who grant it. White feminists are 'everything'. We speak for other groups, rather than letting them speak for themselves. We think of ourselves as experts and sav- iours. We speak of mutual love and happiness with no acknowledgement of our role in the violence of racial capitalism and white supremacy. We appropriate the ideas and politics of non-white people to justify these power games. I have certainly done all these things. If you are a white woman reading this, you have probably done them too.

Critical theorists of whiteness have pointed out the narcissism of white identity.[7] White people see ourselves in everything around us – we bathe in posi- tive images of people with white skin. Political and corporate leaders look like us; celebrities and other public figures do too. Most of us live and work in pre- dominantly white neighbourhoods and communities, which means we hardly, if ever, enter a space in which we don't belong. As Sara Ahmed says, whiteness is a mode of being 'at home' in the world, because it has been made in our image.[8] We don't get stopped at the border. We don't worry about being brutalised by the police. We don't have to deal with ignorant and insen- sitive comments about our whiteness, day in and day out. We don't get called angry and unreasonable when we point racism out.

White people are 'everything'. We see our views as objective, and think our experiences represent those of everyone else. We expect to be centred, even in anti-racist movements. As Robin DiAngelo writes in her famous article 'White Fragility', we stand for humanity. But while whiteness is everything, it is not to be identified – we also see ourselves as profoundly unique individuals. This means we get defensive about our privilege. White people are *just people* and we don't have – or see – race. This individualism, in DiAngelo's words, allows us to distance ourselves from white supremacy and 'demand to be granted the benefit of the doubt'.[9]

Sociologist Gurminder Bhambra has written about 'methodological whiteness' in academia. She developed this concept in response to academic analysis of, and commentary on, Brexit and the election of Trump. It describes how even in progressive scholarship, there is a narcissistic focus on (and universalisation of) the experiences and concerns of white people. There is also an inability to acknowledge the structures and histories of race and racism that have shaped the world.[10] The methodological whiteness of mainstream feminist scholarship was described in the previous chapter – and this underpins the political whiteness of the mainstream Western feminist movement against sexual violence.

This movement makes claims about 'women's victimhood' based on the experiences of bourgeois white women. In 1982, in an article called 'White woman listen!', Marxist feminist scholar Hazel Carby highlighted some of the ways that dominant feminist narratives excluded Black women and other women of colour.[11] For instance, the family is often defined as the primary site of women's oppression. But Black families and other families of colour can also be havens against capitalist and colonial cultures, and sites of alternative modes of social reproduction. The criminal punishment system is usually called on to deal with sexual violence, but this system is fundamentally racist. And white women are still not listening.

Recently, feminists of colour and working-class white feminists have argued that the key preoccupations of the mainstream movement, such as online misogyny, women on banknotes, and banning 'Page 3' topless models or 'Formula 1 girls', are not so crucial for women marginalised by race and/or class. But more pressing issues such as austerity and hostile immigration environments get comparatively little attention. There is narcissism in this white feminist refusal of intersectionality, this privileging of gender over race, class and other categories of oppression. Sometimes the refusal is unwitting and sometimes it is deliberate: in her 1991 essay 'What is a White Woman Anyway?', Catharine MacKinnon argued that white women's subordination had been trivialised by the critiques of women of colour.[12]

White feminist narcissism has no truck with the idea that we are anything but victims. Here is an example: in 2015 there was a white feminist outcry over Rihanna's music video for a track called 'Bitch Better Have My Money'. In the seven-minute film, Rihanna kidnaps the white wife of an accountant who has defrauded her. The woman is bundled into a trunk, stripped, swung upside down from a rope, knocked unconscious with a bottle and left to almost drown in a swimming pool. Following this, Rihanna straps the accountant to a chair and shows him a collection of knives. The end of the film pictures her, naked and covered in blood, in a trunk full of dollar bills. 'Bitch Better Have My Money' upset privileged white feminists.[13] It was misogynist, they said. In the *New Statesman*, Helen Lewis wrote: 'It was not very feminist – not even very hashtag feminist – of Rihanna to "torture that poor rich lady". That is because it is not very feminist to torture women. Even if they are white. Even if they are rich. Even if you are a woman yourself.'

This positioning of Rihanna's video as anti-feminist (perhaps deliberately) ignored its complexities. The video can be interpreted as an intersectional feminist statement (whether Rihanna intended this or not). As Mia McKenzie wrote on her blog *Black Girl Dangerous*, 'Bitch Better Have My Money' was the revenge fantasy of a Black woman exploited by white culture, a culture embodied and perpetuated by white women as well as white men.[14] The video viscerally expressed how Black women are oppressed at the intersections of gender and race. And claims that it was misogynist and anti-feminist were claims to ownership of gender – and feminism – on behalf of white women. Because white women are 'everything', because we stand for *all women*, a revenge fantasy against us is misogynist and anti-feminist, even if it is the fantasy of a woman of colour. This is a study in the 'Me, Not You' of the mainstream feminist movement.

This narcissism is mirrored in the backlash. What about the (white) men? The experience of whiteness as comfort lowers our capacity to tolerate its opposite, especially in the form of being criticised or held accountable. Accountability exposes the deep fragility of whiteness. This can be seen in the use of the phrase 'witch-hunt' about feminist movements against sexual violence. Sometimes they are called 'lynch mobs', which is even worse. This rhetoric equates attempts to hold powerful people to account with the systematic and violent persecution of marginalised groups. It is incredibly narcissistic.

Counter-attack is, then, inevitable. In #MeToo, this took a number of forms: the hashtag #HimToo which identified accused men as victims and advised all men to be scared; men on Wall Street who decided to avoid women at all costs for protection; victim-blaming, chest-beating about 'false allegations', and the rest. And white women joined this outraged chorus: celebrities, libertarian feminists and conservative female commentators all took part in the #MeToo backlash. Actor Catherine Deneuve bemoaned the 'media lynching' of men accused of sexual harassment. Journalist Melanie Phillips opined that it was 'time vilified men had their #MeToo'.

The instinct to counter-attack in response to narcissistic wounding shapes reactionary movements dominated by white people. It produces scorn for 'identity politics', even while it creates its own identity politics to justify defending entitlements and hoarding resources. It makes white people want to 'take our country back' or 'make it great again'. And this instinct to counter-attack is shared by white feminists. In her famous account of race in the feminist movement, Audre Lorde highlights how white women often answer Black women's anger about racism with our own. We tell Black women they are creating negativity or preventing us from getting past our guilt. We continually (re)centre ourselves. Lorde recounts reading from her work entitled 'Poems for Women in Rage' and being asked by a white woman, 'are you going to do anything with how we can deal directly with *our* anger? I feel it's so important.'[15]

## The white self as wounded self

The narcissistic self is a wounded self. The backlash against #MeToo was obsessed with the 'wounds' of accused men, as well as those of the movement's critics. Author and journalist Katie Roiphe, who had been a key figure in the 1990s opposition to sexual violence activism on US campuses, penned an article in *Harper's Magazine* called 'The Other Whisper Network'. In it, she claimed that #MeToo's detractors were so afraid of recriminations they were being silenced. 'Can you see why some of us are whispering?', she asked. 'It is the sense of viciousness lying in wait, of violent hate just waiting to be unfurled, that leads people to keep their opinions to themselves, or to share them only with close friends.'

Statements like this locate violence in the fight against, rather than the fact of, oppression. They reflect what William C. Anderson and Zoe Samudzi call a false equivalence between domination and resistance, which has long been a feature of colonial systems.[16] The rhetoric of reverse victimisation is also strengthened at a time when the 'wounds' of the right have come to dominate public debate in many Western countries. As the right wages war against 'gender ideology', feminism becomes the oppressor while men whose sexual entitlement is challenged become oppressed. As Trump said to reporters during the Kavanaugh hearings: 'it's a scary time for young men in America'.

The 'wounds' of this backlash predominate even though it also criticises women and feminists for engaging in 'victim' or 'grievance' politics. Germaine Greer famously characterised #MeToo as 'whingeing'. In *The Spectator*, commentator Joanna Williams interpreted it as 'an unedifying clamour to be included in celebrity suffering'. But although they pretend to decry victimhood, statements like this are really a petulant howl about whose wounds are worse. Who is really being victimised by all this talk of victimhood? This right-wing victim/anti-victim rhetoric often emerges in response to feminist movements against sexual violence.

Whiteness is predisposed to woundedness. As author and journalist Reni Eddo-Lodge says, whiteness is a position of structural power concerned with maintaining that power.[17] From a position of power, one is naturally preoccupied with threat. The feudal lord, the factory owner, the settler, the master, the financier, the oligarch and the tycoon – these are all emblems of conquest and subjugation. And there is always a risk that they will be displaced or violently overthrown. Whether from peasants, trades unions, Indigenous or enslaved populations, immigrants, 'political correctness', 'identity politics' or 'social justice warriors', the idea of privileged whiteness under threat has significant cultural influence. And 'victim politics' is victimisation because it means consequences for dominant groups accustomed to acting with impunity.

In this way, white woundedness reflects white supremacy: lost entitlement becomes victimisation. On International Men's Day 2019, *Good Morning Britain* host Piers Morgan ushered in the celebrations with a monologue comparing bourgeois white men to endangered rhinos. 'Yes, we do need a day', he said. 'We are now the most downtrodden group of men in the world.' White feminists have generally (and rightly) given such statements short shrift. In 2014, following a series of attacks from men's rights activists, feminist writer Jessica Valenti tweeted a picture of herself wearing a T-shirt that read 'I BATHE IN MALE TEARS.'

But what about female tears? White female tears, to be exact? White fragility has also been noted in feminist politics, often becoming most obvious in conversations about race. And tears have pride of place. Mamta

Accapadi and Ruby Hamad are among many feminists
of colour who have described how white feminists use
tears to deflect and avoid accountability in difficult discussions and situations.[18] White feminist tears deploy
white woundedness, and the sympathy it generates, to
hide the harms we perpetrate through white supremacy. These tears are not just personal; they are political too. In 2019 Theresa May cried as she resigned the
UK premiership. And her tears did political work: they
seemed to create collective amnesia over the abuses
she enabled as Prime Minister, and before that as
Home Secretary. Even the charity Women's Aid posted
a (now deleted) tweet thanking May for everything she
had done for women and survivors.

Just prior to her resignation, May had failed to guar-
antee that women's refuges would not close due to government plans for an overhaul of supported housing. In
2015 she was accused of allowing the 'state-sanctioned'
rape and abuse of vulnerable migrant women at the
Yarl's Wood detention centre.[19] Her government presided over the rollout of universal credit, a punitive
benefits system that has pushed many people further
into poverty and made it more difficult for women
to leave abusive relationships. In 2019 May's government rendered Shamima Begum stateless: Begum was
one of three London teenagers who travelled to join
Daesh in 2015, and was found in 2019, nine months
pregnant, in a refugee camp in northern Syria (her baby
subsequently died). These acts, and many others, were
washed away by May's tears. And the power of 'white

tears' still reflects white privilege even when – as in
the case of #MeToo – those tears are shed over real
experiences of trauma.

Water was a powerful metaphor for #MeToo. The
movement was described as a 'flood' of stories of
sexual assault by CNN, CBS and CBC, and a 'tsunami'
on CNBC, in the *Times of India*, the *New York Times*
and the US *National Post*. These metaphors for natural disaster were used by supporters and critics alike,
and have also been used about other viral feminist
movements such as #BeenRapedNeverReported. They
evoked trauma on a massive scale. They also, arguably,
constructed sexual violence as an inevitable 'force of
nature', tapping into established patriarchal myths.
They also represented the movement as a collective
weeping, a release of (white) tears.

White women's tears are powerful, the ultimate
symbol of femininity. They evoke the damsel in
distress and the mourning, lamenting women of
myth. In Greek mythology, Niobe wept unceasingly
after her children were killed by Artemis and Apollo;
even after being turned to stone, tears poured from her
petrified face. Penelope in Homer's *Odyssey* waited
for her husband Odysseus for two decades in her 'bed
of sorrows', which she watered with tears until she
fell asleep. In an article on #MeToo, Jamilah Lemieux
commented: 'white women know how to be victims.
They know just how to bleed and weep in the public
square, they fundamentally understand that they are
entitled to sympathy.'[20]

Lemieux was not saying that the tears of #MeToo were not genuine (and neither am I). But the cultural power of mainstream feminism is linked to the cultural power of white tears. This power elevates the lost entitlements of the backlash, the wounded whiteness of the far right, *and* white women's deeply felt pain about sexual violence. These injuries (or perceived injuries, in the case of reactionary politics) are not equivalent. But they are all transmitted to the world through the channels of race and class power. Mainstream feminist activism against sexual violence is shaped and communicated by the woundedness of white bourgeois femininity. And although this woundedness may date back to the ancients, it was solidified – and sexualised – in the modern colonial period.

## White femininity and sexualised threat

Colonialism was both gendered and sexualised. To justify its existence, it relied on various dichotomies that blended ideas about gender, sexuality, class and race. For instance, between the 'respectable' white bourgeois family and the 'degeneracy' of Indigenous communities. And between the 'pure, fragile, innocent' white woman and the 'sexual savagery' of people of colour. Protecting white women was, and is, a key colonial preoccupation. Imaginings of Indigenous and/or slave uprisings were sexualised: fear of revolution was fear of rape.[21] In colonial and neo-colonial cultures, white women's tears are deadly to people of colour.

This 'risk' posed to white women from the oversexu-
alised Other has justified racist community and state
violence, both historically and now. It has justified the
violent subjugation and genocide of Indigenous communities, who were invested with 'depraved' sexual
urges and often with 'mutilated' or 'oversized' geni-
tals. It has justified the lynching of Black men and
boys – for instance, 14-year-old Emmett Till. Till was
brutalised and killed by two white men in Mississippi
in 1955, after Carolyn Bryant accused him of 'utter-
ing obscenities' and grabbing her by the waist.[22] In an
interview in 2008, Bryant admitted that she had lied –
Bryant's 'white lie' cost a Black boy his life. Sociologist
Jessie Daniels has called Bryant 'the foremother of contemporary white women who call the police on black
people sitting in a Starbucks, barbecuing in a park or
napping in a dorm', acts that have also led to fatal
violence.[23] It's no wonder Black women have revenge
fantasies about us.

While bourgeois white women such as Bryant are seen
as innocent victims of sexual violence, women marginalised by race and/or class are blamed for causing it.
The virgin/whore dichotomy is classed and raced. And
for Black women, the always-willingness they have
been assigned reflects what Saidiya Hartman describes
as a rupture between Blackness and consent that
occurred in the context of slavery.[24] The 'Jezebel' stereotype legitimated the rape of enslaved Black women,
which expressed and maintained white supremacy and
reproduced generations of enslaved people. And the

stereotype endures. In 2017 a Georgetown Law Center report found that Black girls are still less likely to be believed when they report rape, because they are seen as 'less innocent' than their white peers.[25]

In 1971 philosopher and essayist Susan Griffin wrote: 'I have never been free of the fear of rape.'[26] Forty-seven years later, novelist Barbara Kingsolver wrote: 'If the #MeToo revolution has proved anything, it's that women live under threat. Not sometimes, but all the time.'[27] This imperilled femininity is white. It depends on tropes of racist domination, even while it articulates the gendered harm of sexual violence. It is the white woman weeping in the public square. It is Niobe and Penelope. It is Carolyn Bryant. In contrast, Jamilah Lemieux argues, Black women 'know that [they] need to tuck that shit in and keep moving'. This robustness expected of Black women (and their working-class white sisters) reflects raced and classed histories: less privileged women have headed households, performed manual and agricultural labour and endured much harsher living conditions, including, of course, being enslaved.

Black women's assumed ability to 'bear the lash' (to quote Sojourner Truth) sets off the symbolic woundedness of privileged white femininity. The sexually endangered bourgeois white woman is the foil to the Black woman's status as un-rapeable, and can also be juxtaposed with constructions of other women of colour, for instance that of the 'brown' (and usually Muslim) woman, who is always already wounded but very rarely allowed to speak. She is often desexualised, and seen as sexually oppressed. She is used, with the support of colonial feminists, to fortify the white saviourism of colonial and neo-colonial projects. In this process, she is spoken for by privileged white women – we appropriate her tears as our own, to gain platforms and power for ourselves.

The figure of the sexually endangered white woman also shapes the emphasis on sexual behaviour, rather than structural power, in contemporary mainstream feminism. This has often been termed 'prudish' and 'anti-sex' by detractors both within and outside the movement. Of course, this is an easy way for libertarian reactionaries to dismiss feminist ideas. But since the 'sex wars' of the late 1970s there have been lively debates *between* feminists about the status of sex and sexuality in analyses of gender. Are we concerned with sexual oppression or sexual repression? Are we rejecting sexism or sex? These questions persist, especially as they affect more marginalised groups such as sex workers and queer and trans people.

Some commentators on #MeToo remarked that sex appeared to have overshadowed harassment. For journalist Melissa Gira Grant, the increasingly popular term 'sexual misconduct' tended to evoke the interpersonal rather than the systemic and gave the impression that women were asking to be insulated from sex rather than objecting to abuses of power.[28] Others were concerned that the focus on sex could feed a 'moral panic' around sexual behaviour which could disproportionately impact queer communities and/or sex workers, as had happened in the past. As gender scholar Jane Ward wrote:

> These are common dyke stories: being the first sus-
> pect when sexual misbehavior is (or is imagined to be)
> afoot; being told to stay away from the children in one's
> extended family; keeping your distance in locker rooms
> and bathrooms and other places where straight women
> presume the absence of same-sex desire and panic
> when they realize it could present. Dykes know what it
> means to be the accused.[29]

Dykes know what it means to be the accused. And an emphasis on sexual behaviour rather than structural power means that those whose bodies are automatically sexualised – people marginalised by race and/or sexuality, people who sell sex – may be at risk if mainstream feminist activism crosses into, or feeds, moral panic.

### 'Taking back control' – the white will to power

The structural power of whiteness creates a sense of victimhood when entitlements and powers are threatened, as seen in backlash and ethno-nationalist forms of white politics. White victimhood also produces the desire to 'take back control' – a slogan that has been at the forefront of far-right politics in many different countries. Campaigners for the UK to leave the European Union used exactly this slogan, repeatedly and relentlessly. Americans elected Trump to 'Make

America Great Again' (a slogan echoed in Spain – and about Spain – in 2018 by the far-right party Vox).

Similarly, the backlash against feminism often claims that it has 'gone too far', a clarion call for men to regain their rightful place in the gender order. In more mainstream circles this is expressed as concern that men are now the downtrodden sex. Online, men's rights activists combine rape and death threats with instructions to 'make [them] a sandwich'. In the incel mindset, mass murder is an appropriate response to not being able to get a date.

As white feminists, we are well acquainted with the white man's will to power. We bathe in male tears. But the white will to power can also exist as whiteness intersects with gender inequalities and with individual experiences of victimisation. White women, and survivors of sexual violence, can possess and express it too. Indeed, gender may intensify it: as Lugones argues, white women's investments in white supremacy partly reflect our lack of control, within capitalism, over the means of production.[30] It's also possible that sexual violence might intensify the will to power: since sexual violence involves a loss of power and control, regaining this becomes crucial to recovery.

Survivors of sexual violence are encouraged to 'take back control' of our lives in various ways, from making our own decisions about reporting and support, to when and whether to engage in consensual sex afterwards, to going back to work or college.[31] We are sometimes advised to make small changes to experience a sense of restored control, for instance cutting our hair. All this is entirely sensible and necessary. But when the personal becomes political, regaining control can also be expressed through a focus on 'taking down' powerful men.

Weinstein, Nassar, Spacey. Diaz, Dreyfuss, Depardieu. Franco, Copperfield, Stallone. The 'shitty media men'. Tarana Burke, as founder of #MeToo, has consistently critiqued its focus on 'bad men' like these. 'The conversation is largely about Harvey Weinstein or other individual bogeymen', she said in a 2017 interview. 'No matter how much I keep talking about power and privilege, they keep bringing it back to individuals.'[32] Burke's caution about 'bringing down' men such as Weinstein is not about shielding them from accountability. Instead, it is rooted in the knowledge that systems of oppression intersect. It expresses the Black feminist concern that strengthening punitive systems will not generally affect privileged white men such as these.

This is a concern that white feminists do not need to share. We have little need to fear the criminal punishment system, and it shows. In 2016 American college student Brock Turner was convicted of sexually assaulting Chanel Miller after she passed out behind a dumpster. Some feminists protested the leniency of his six-month sentence. One response was a bill passed in the California State Legislature to impose a mandatory minimum sentence of three years for sexual assault of an unconscious victim. But Black feminists and other feminists of colour pointed out that mandatory minimums hurt their communities. 'Here's the thing with mandatory minimums', wrote Meg Sri in *Feministing*, 'they were designed to prop up the exact same system that cut Turner loose, and put a vast swath of people of color in droves behind bars.'[33]

Then Vice President Joe Biden was fêted by white feminists after an open letter to Miller (then known as Emily Doe) sharing his 'furious anger' at what she had been through. Biden's righteous anger has made him a feminist hero before. He was the lead Senate sponsor of the 1994 Crime Bill, which mandated more funding for police and prisons, more 'three-strikes' laws, an expansion of the death penalty and less money to help incarcerated people access education. Mainstream feminists supported this draconian bill, because it also contained the Violence Against Women Act. Biden is a hero of carceral feminism, which is undeniably white.

For white feminists, criminal punishment represents protection, not oppression. It is the colonial master's intervention, the 'empathy' of Angry Dad. It is also the indirect demonstration of our own will to power. (Mostly) lacking legitimate authority and economic power in a still-patriarchal world, we 'take back control' by *ceding control* to the punitive technologies of the state. (And we really do cede control: survivors have been arrested and prosecuted for refusing to testify or otherwise cooperate with carceral agendas.) And as the far right makes parliamentary gains, as fascists weaponise 'women's safety' against marginalised groups, mainstream feminism stays focused on state remedies for personal harm. The dominant conversation about sexual violence remains one between white women and white men, about who is more wounded and who is in control.

Its cosy relationship with the state means that mainstream feminism tends to ignore issues such as police brutality and endemic sexual violence in prisons. These issues are forfeit to the project of protecting white women from sexual threat. Also forfeit are sexual violence survivors who do not meet the standards of bourgeois whiteness, who need to be criminalised 'for their own good'. For instance, sex workers. Mainstream feminists – including many of the Hollywood women at the forefront of #MeToo – tend to support approaches to sex industry regulation that criminalise sex workers directly or indirectly, and make them more vulnerable to violence (migrant sex workers especially).[34] These policies are supported in the service of challenging men's sexual entitlement and 'keeping women safe'. Which women? You might well ask.

This sacrificing of more marginalised people is another way that #MeToo can become 'Me, Not You'. Political whiteness is the systematic privileging of bourgeois white women's wounds *at the expense of others*. Its obsession with threat is both sexualised and racialised, because of the role of colonialism in co-constructing race and sexuality. And in keeping with the nihilism of white supremacy, threats have to be eradicated in any way possible. This reveals both political and emotional splitting: one can be a victim or a perpetrator, but one cannot be both. Bad men are bad men. White feminists rarely, if ever, look at ourselves: instead, we spend a lot of our time in outrage about the misdeeds of other people.

# Chapter 4

# The outrage economy

Feminism underpinned by political whiteness seeks power within the existing system, not the overthrow of the system itself. This is 'lean-in' corporate feminism, and the governance feminism that has put 'femocrats' in local, national and international bureaucracies. This feminism advocates for women on banknotes, but does not necessarily dispute the hands that the majority of these banknotes are in. It sees both Sheryl Sandberg and Hillary Clinton, with their investments in racial capitalism and militarism, as icons of women's success. It consumes ideas of diversity and inclusion as if the playing field is level underneath. But its slogans – 'Girl Power!', 'This is What a Feminist Looks Like!' – appear on T-shirts made by abused and underpaid female sweatshop workers in the Global South. Mainstream feminism leans in to both the punitive state and the capitalist economy.

Mainstream feminism also operates with its own economies. Sarah Banet-Weiser's book *Empowered* explores the economy of visibility that both popular feminism and popular misogyny participate in, in a media-driven world. Its key currencies are views, clicks, likes and shares. Success is being *seen*, getting the spotlight. And it often stops there, 'as if *seeing* or purchasing feminism is the same thing as changing patriarchal structures'.[1] This preoccupation with being seen reflects the narcissism of political whiteness. And it befits the self-referential way we communicate, in networked media and social media environments.

We are now living in an era of what political theorist Jodi Dean calls 'communicative capitalism', marked by a proliferation of communications that do not actually communicate much. As content circulates and recirculates, generating clicks, likes and shares, messages rarely impact on official politics. Instead, influential people and organisations circulate their own communications. In communicative capitalism, there is not a lot of listening. Transmission, rather than discussion, is the order of the day. And although transmissions primarily function to generate value for media markets, we understand them as democracy. 'Ideals of access, inclusion, discussion and participation', Dean writes, are now realised through 'expansions, intensifications and interconnections of global telecommunications'. This has created a mass of communications jostling for dominance.[2]

One of the ways dominance is achieved is particularly relevant to the mainstream feminist movement – the method of generating outrage. 'Outrage media' has long been a feature of the political right, described by social scientists Berry and Sobieraj as containing 'venom, vilification of opponents, and hyperbolic rein-terpretations of current events'.[3] The 'shock jock' and his equivalents have been around for a while. And the global shift rightwards, together with the proliferation of networked and social media, has created a genera-tion of modern 'shock jocks' and audiences hungry for agitation. The Howard Sterns have been joined by online demagogues such as Alex Jones and PewDiePie.

The contemporary right makes excellent use of out-rage. The script is always the same: 1) say something outrageous; 2) wait for outrage to build; 3) claim to be silenced and no-platformed; 4) build platform from outrage this generates; 5) start all over again. We have seen countless 'alt'-right 'provocateurs', from Milo Yiannopoulos to Jordan Peterson, make their names using this method. I have also seen the same tech-niques used by some white feminists – usually 'gender critical' or trans-exclusionary ones – who are able to generate additional outrage by calling their critics misogynists. These manoeuvres manipulate outrage to get attention and build a brand. And as well as building individual brands, outrage is central to contemporary right-wing political movements. It provides a space where politics as content circulation and politics as official activity can meet. White outrage about immi-gration was manipulated, at scale, by far-right figures and parties in the lead-up to the Brexit referendum and the election of Trump.

And in the US, the UK and elsewhere, far-right nar-ratives are beginning to dominate conservative media outlets, and take up increasing amounts of space in liberal ones under the pretext of 'balanced debate'. Structural changes in the networked media landscape have also made generating clickbait a priority, across the board.[4] I call this the 'outrage economy' of contemporary media, and it intersects with the economy of visibility that Banet-Weiser describes.

## The performativity of outrage

Progressive movements, as well as reactionary ones, have been built on outrage. As broadcaster Ashley 'Dotty' Charles has written, outrage 'has fought against police brutality, institutional racism, unequal pay … conquered apartheid and abolished slavery'.[5] It has also been a key weapon in the fight against sexual violence. Outrage about the widely sanctioned rape of Black women by white men was central to the Civil Rights movement. Reclaim the Night started in the UK in 1977 because feminists in Leeds were outraged about police telling them to stay indoors while the 'Yorkshire Ripper' Peter Sutcliffe was on the loose.

Outrage is cathartic. It has righteousness because of its 'outness': it takes up space, demands attention to the matter at hand. It can put us in touch with our feelings about issues; it can be a collective release. In the information overload of communicative capitalism, the spotlight of outrage stops us feeling so helpless. But information overload can also create a fuzzy abundance of outrage that does not translate into action.

We are outraged about something; we are outraged about something else. Sometimes, it seems that everybody is outraged but nobody is quite sure about what. Sometimes, the catharsis of outrage might be an end in itself.

Outrage can be connective, a way of showing support. We can use it to say: 'I am with you.' We can use it to say: 'It wasn't your fault.' In a world where sexual violence survivors are routinely dismissed and disbelieved, outrage is necessary. It is an antidote to the 'second rape' that occurs within communities, institutions and criminal punishment systems, in which the victim is judged and called a liar.[6] If outrage is withheld, survivors are left with their guilt and shame. As someone who was raped in a small community that mostly either ignored the incident or closed ranks around the perpetrator, I understand this very well.

Outrage is a statement: *this is not OK.* When we do outrage, we take a stand. The petition, the open letter and the hashtag are key tools of contemporary outrage. But useful as these are, they are statements and not discussions; they are the circulating transmissions of the communicative capitalist age. They also create and rely on a chorus, to bring movements together: a homogeneous, and infectious, emotional response. This risks outrage becoming performative. Especially on social media, we can get our rage out to fit in. When a big issue is on the table there can be a sense that if you are not performing outrage, you are doing something wrong. And then outrage becomes political whiteness, a rapid ego-boost in a transmission-focused media economy.

The performativity of outrage may be one reason why it blows over. We sign the petition or the open letter; we post using the hashtag; we have done our bit. Especially for those not directly affected by issues or involved in campaigns, outrage can be performed without any other action being required. Information technology does the work for us, turning complex problems into soundbites and offering a quick fix.[7] Sometimes, such actions work: in 2019 Cambridge University sacked researcher Noah Carl after an open letter signed by more than 1,000 scholars said that his work stoked racist, xenophobic, fascist and anti-immigration rhetoric.[8] And after an outcry about his role in the Flint water crisis, former Michigan Governor Rick Snyder withdrew from a fellowship at Harvard.[9] But often, actions don't work. In 2016 a Pew Research Center study examined the site *We The People*, which allowed Americans to petition the Obama administration. It found only three instances where petitioning led to concrete policy outcomes, even though there were a total of 38.5 million signatures on more than 473,000 petitions.[10]

In 2018 *Elle UK* ran an article on five feminist petitions its readers could sign to commemorate International Women's Day. The selling point was that this action would take less than five minutes.[11] Online activism is often disparagingly called 'clicktivism' or 'slacktivism', in a way that has more to do with older generations dismissing younger than with genuine political critique. It also ignores the fact that for community and political organisers, online actions are usually one part of a broader strategy. We must not forget the key role of social media in important movements such as the Arab Spring and Black Lives Matter. But for those of us not involved in organising, the personal gratification of signing a petition or posting on a hashtag *can be* the primary or only outcome. This is how, as Dean argues, communicative capitalism *prevents* politicisation.

In 2014 276 Nigerian schoolgirls were kidnapped in the town of Chibok by the group Jama'atu Ahlis Sunna Lidda'awati wal-Jihad (commonly known as Boko Haram). In response, and in protest at the lack of government intervention, Abuja lawyer Ibrahim Abdullahi started the hashtag #BringBackOurGirls. It trended globally, and was picked up by a number of Western politicians, celebrities and feminists. In Nigeria and across the African diaspora, support for the hashtag was associated with offline actions and broader critiques of the Goodluck Jonathan administration, the economic effects of colonialism and the continued expansion of Western corporations. But Western engagement tended to consist of little more than feel-good postings, or colonial feminist demands that Western military power be mobilised in rescue.[12]

Celebrities such as Cara Delevigne and Alexa Chung, and political figures such as Michelle Obama, took selfies with 'Bring Back Our Girls' written on placards (or in Chung's case, a mirror), prompting a wave of imitations online. And while there were non-white women involved, this show of Western empathy and outrage on behalf of schoolgirls brutalised 'over there' seemed steeped in political whiteness, not least because of the format the pictures were in. As Nigerian-American writer Teju Cole tweeted: 'Remember: #BringBackOurGirls, a vital moment for Nigerian democracy, is not the same as #BringBackOurGirls, a wave of global sentimentality.' And when the girls were not rescued or returned, most Western feminists moved on.

In 2000 scholar Lauren Berlant asked: 'What does it mean for the theory and practice of social transformation when *feeling good* becomes evidence of justice's triumph?'[13] One answer is that we can feel compelled to 'take a stand' without thinking more deeply about the stand we are taking. Sometimes our stand is self-serving. Sometimes it is harmful. In 2019 the US state of Georgia banned abortions after six weeks' gestation, effectively a total ban. In response, 50 Hollywood actors, including Alyssa Milano, Sean Penn, Alec Baldwin, Sophie Turner and Jessica Chastain, signed a letter pledging to boycott filming in states with strict abortion legislation. But Black feminists pointed out that this would mostly hurt marginalised Black women, who were also key targets of the punitive abortion ban. As Twitter user @YesAurielle wrote: 'My city is filled w/Black working class ppl. The health of the film industry very much affects the food, rideshare, folks who do childcare, and other related markets. Can you guess who's all up & through them industries? Black. Working class. Birthing folks.'

'Taking a stand' on popular issues can also mask our own complicity in oppression. I am thinking of Theresa May's 'This is What a Feminist Looks Like' T-shirt, worn while her government cut funding for women's refuges and presided over abuse at Yarl's Wood. I am thinking of New York Governor Andrew Cuomo, a key partner of Time's Up, who for eight years in a row has refused to use his powers of clemency to free criminalised survivors in his state. I am thinking of actor James Franco, who wore a 'Time's Up' pin to the 2018 Golden Globes, which prompted a number of women to come forward with complaints about *his* behaviour.[14] I am thinking of Sean Penn's alleged history of domestic abuse. These are high-profile examples, but outrage can be camouflage for all of us. It keeps our focus on the 'bad men' and stops us looking at ourselves.

## Trauma as investment

Generating outrage is an excellent way of generating clicks, likes and shares. Outrage is a form of capital that can be accumulated in these currencies, to gain visibility and attention and/or to further a political cause. And how do we generate the capital of outrage? We need something outrageous to invest. The contemporary value of outrage is perhaps one reason for the current proliferation and success of 'fake news'. Did you hear that Black Lives Matter created a blockade to stop aid getting to Hurricane Harvey victims? Or that Alexandria Ocasio-Cortez opposes Daylight Savings Time, because the extra hour of sunlight speeds up climate change?

Feminists are not known for creating fake news. Our outrage tends to be inspired by real injustices we experience or perceive. But we have another form of investment capital, and that is trauma. Contemporary networked media and popular culture are 'testimonial' and affective spaces in which, perhaps in place of politics, discussions have been saturated with feeling.[15] Increasingly, and along with many others, we 'invest' our personal pain in media markets. The phrases 'disaster porn' and 'tragedy porn' have been coined to describe our fascination with the troubles of others, whether this is the 'flood' of sexual violence stories during #MeToo or the photographs of drowned migrants at the border.[16] This 'porn' allows us the quick fix of empathy and outrage, but does not often lead to sustained protest or systemic analysis. It wins reporters and photographers Pulitzer Prizes; it makes media outlets money.

#MeToo generated outrage through sharing stories of sexual violence alongside 'naming and shaming' alleged perpetrators. This was a movement of communicative capitalism, seeing justice in media exposure (despite the fact that public shaming has been a key tool of patriarchal oppression throughout history).[17] Its communications also generated revenue. I have no idea how much, but I would be willing to bet that the profits, especially from high-profile 'scoops', outstripped the costs of dealing with men *within* media industries accused of sexual harassment and abuse. The *New York Times* estimates that #MeToo 'brought down' 201 powerful men, following at least 920 allegations. I cannot even imagine what all that coverage is worth.

Naming and shaming is not restricted to #MeToo: sexual violence campaigns in universities and other institutions have also used this mode of 'speaking out', often when 'speaking in' has failed. Media disclosure can be a last resort when an institution, employer or community has profoundly let you down – scholars Tiffany Page, Anna Bull and Emma Chapman argue that in situations like this, naming and shaming is direct action.[18] It can also feel like justice, because the media are eager for this:

CAMBRIDGE DON ACCUSED OF SEXUAL HARASSMENT UNDER INVESTIGATION AGAIN

STANFORD LINEBACKER WAS ACCUSED OF RAPE BEFORE GOING ON TO NFL

HARVEY WEINSTEIN SCANDAL: WHO HAS ACCUSED HIM OF WHAT?

But media markets, like all markets, are profoundly nihilistic. Clicks, likes and shares are a multi-denominational currency. As long as they accumulate, as long as visibility (and revenue) is gained, it does not matter why. In other words, the media using sexual violence as clickbait does not imply support for feminist goals. Using sexual violence as clickbait does not mean survivors will not themselves be vilified if this happens to be the better story. Because the media are also eager for this:

'SORRY DOESN'T CUT IT' – STUDENT FALSELY ACCUSED OF RAPE WAS 'DRAGGED THROUGH HELL' AFTER BUNGLING COPS WITHHELD TEXTS FROM 'VICTIM' BEGGING FOR SEX

FRAT RAPE ACCUSER LIED FOR #METOO FAME

'I WILL RUIN YOU'. CAMBRIDGE DON WAS CLEARED OF ASSAULTING HIS CHEATING FIANCÉE AFTER SHE MADE UP THE STORY TO RUIN HIM, A COURT HEARS

This is not a critique of the brave survivors who disclose in media outlets. We all seek justice as best we can, and the options are usually pretty slim. And sometimes naming and shaming works. But this is because disclosures in media markets bump up against other, PR-driven sectors, in which institutions and organisations are focused on brand protection. Here, outrage usually brings negative value – it threatens the value of the brand. And the response to naming and shaming is often what I call 'institutional airbrushing': neoliberal institutions and organisations obsessed with how things *look* rather than how they *are* merely remove the 'blemish' that has been exposed. And this impulse to airbrush, rather than tackle problems head-on, is exacerbated by the dogged nihilism of media outrage. When institutions *do* take systemic actions such as putting sexual violence reporting systems in place (and reports increase as a result), they often singled out as having a 'rape problem'.

Sexual harassers and abusers are named and shamed, and then airbrushed out of organisations and institutions while the structural problems that enabled the harassment and abuse remain. Indeed, the language of outrage – of predators who need to be punished – tends to distract from these structures and the generalised toxicity they produce. The culprit often moves on, to continue the same behaviour in a new job. This is called the 'pass the harasser' problem, and it is a particular issue in academia and other high-status professions.[19] It is a direct result of prioritising brand reputation over social justice. It also makes me wonder how many of the men who lost their jobs because of #MeToo continue to harass and assault women elsewhere, perhaps in lower-status sectors, where women have less support and fewer employment rights.

This is mainstream sexual violence activism in a capitalist context. We 'invest' our trauma in networked media markets, to generate outrage and the visibility we need to further our cause. Cynical media corporations exploit this outrage, building visibility for their brands through clicks, likes and shares by encouraging audiences to consume our pain. Meanwhile the threat of damage, through widespread outrage, to the brands of exposed institutions and organisations leads to a purging of 'bad men' from high-profile sectors. These individuals may well move on to start all over again, while dysfunctional systems are left intact. Although this is not our intention, this seems more like NIMBYism to me than radical political action. Although this is not our intention, I'm afraid this is the 'Me, Not You' of political whiteness.[20]

Media outrage can also exacerbate the punitive tendencies of political whiteness. In 2017 sexual misconduct by UK academics was described as an 'epidemic', following a freedom of information investigation of 300 universities by the *Observer* newspaper. Fittingly, the description itself spread rapidly, with the word 'epidemic' used by many outlets including the *Telegraph*, the *Independent*, the *International Business Times*, student magazine *The Tab*, the *University Times* and the *Huffington Post*. The *Observer* investigation actually uncovered an average of less than half an allegation per institution, per year. However, to deal with the problem, recommendations were made including a strict 'no-contact' rule between staff and students, the penalty for violating which would be a 'swift termination with a public statement and a mandated report to a central UK registry'.[21]

The impulse to punish in response to outrage produced a key tension in #MeToo between the desire to expose the 'everydayness' of sexual violence, and the outcome which was the 'bringing down' of a number of individual men. While we get our rage out, we want its subject out – out of our institutions, out of our communities, out of society for good. We want Harvey Weinstein in prison. We want Brock Turner to have a longer sentence. We want Judge Aquilina to sign Nassar's death warrant. We rely on a third party to take these 'bad men' away, usually in the form of an institution or the state. And this White Knight or Angry Dad is patriarchy personified. This is how our outraged activism fails to dismantle the intersecting systems of heteropatriarchy and racial capitalism that produce sexual violence – and strengthens them instead.

## Pricing Others out[22]

The successful investment of trauma as capital often relies on other capitals. The bourgeois, white and Western women at the forefront of movements against sexual violence tend to have benefited, rather than suffered, from the economic shifts that have created a massive expansion of electronic communications. We are comfortable in political realms that have much in common with advertising and PR. We have the cultural and social capital needed to access media platforms.

Because of this, our trauma can easily be used to generate outrage. The trauma of more marginalised women cannot, unless we speak for them (which we very often do). Women marginalised because of race, class, sexual orientation, gender identity, disability and age are often 'priced out' of the outrage economy. And unfortunately, if they challenge the tenets of mainstream feminism, this pricing out can be deliberate.

I have a complex and ambivalent relationship with the mainstream feminist movement. Because of this, my comrades and teachers have not just been women like me: they have been women of colour, trans women and sex workers, and women who fit two or more of these descriptors (you know who you are). These women understand the systemic causes of sexual violence because they live at the harsh ends of oppressive systems. But despite their experience and expertise they are often belittled and their trauma denied, by white feminist academics, journalists, politicians and others. In the process these privileged women use their own pain as capital, or co-opt that of others, to advance their political agendas. This is especially noticeable in debates about sex workers' rights and transgender inclusion.

In sex industry debates, feminists opposed to the industry often speak for women who have left it. Catharine MacKinnon and Andrea Dworkin (herself an ex sex worker) made the voices of Linda Lovelace and other exploited women central to their 1980s campaign for an Anti-pornography Civil Rights Ordinance. Since then, 'survivor stories' about pornography, prostitution and trafficking have acquired corporate gloss and wider exposure, as they are used by groups lobbying for an end to commercial sex. These stories are harrowing accounts of victimisation and suffering. They include physical and sexual violence, problematic substance use, unwanted pregnancy and sexually transmitted infections. They speak to the incredible difficulties that sex workers face in a gendered, stigmatised and criminalised sector. They also (understandably) provoke outrage. But this outrage is often manipulated to support policies that sex workers themselves oppose.

In 2015 Amnesty International issued a draft policy in support of decriminalising sex work. This provoked an immediate outcry from a number of feminists, characterised by various high-profile calls to 'listen to survivors'. A petition by the Coalition Against Trafficking in Women (CATW), signed by over 12,000 people, was endorsed by several Hollywood actors including Meryl Streep, Kate Winslet, Emma Thompson and Anne Hathaway. This petition claimed that Amnesty had decided to 'stand with exploiters, not the exploited', despite the fact that an overwhelming number of sex workers supported the Amnesty policy.

Amnesty's opponents also claimed that the survivors they were speaking for had been 'strategically sidelined' by a movement for decriminalisation headed by 'Johns' and 'pimps'. 'No Amnesty for Pimps!' they cried. Jessica Neuwirth, co-founder of the international NGO Equality Now, said Amnesty had been 'hijacked by proponents of the global sex trade' into supporting 'pimps and buyers of sex'. On social media, the Amnesty logo was edited to replace the lit candle with an ejaculating penis. The outrage reached such a fever pitch that Amnesty's Senior Director for Campaigns, Thomas Schultz-Jagow, was forced to clarify, in the *New York Times*, that the organisation's motives were to protect sex workers and nobody else. Nevertheless, when Amnesty's policy was eventually approved in 2016, CATW issued a press release entitled 'It's Official

– Amnesty International Creates the Human Right to Pimp and Purchase Sexual Acts.'[23]

Anti-sex-industry feminism makes excellent use of outrage. This is generated, quite rightly, in response to the trauma of sex industry survivors. But the telling of survivor stories works in tandem with the idea of a 'pimp lobby', which positions sex workers and their allies as malign. This strategy is very effective: it means that people who support decriminalisation, many of whom are sex workers and/or feminists, are not only failing to 'listen to survivors' but are supporting 'pimps' instead. Sometimes we become pimps ourselves. In 2018 a media outrage campaign was started by anti-sex-industry feminists because a sex worker outreach project had a stand at my university's freshers' fair. After the story broke, I received an anonymous email accusing me of 'pimping out students' from my office.

Anti-sex-industry feminism epitomises political whiteness. The figure of the 'pimp' is racialised: in popular culture, he is often a Black man in hip hop clothing or a zoot suit.[24] He evokes colonial anxieties about violent men of colour who need to be contained through criminal punishment and community violence. And in contrast to the pimp, we are asked to listen to and protect the (implicitly whitened) sex industry survivor. We are also asked to protect the legions of other (white) women at risk because the sex industry commodifies the female body. This is the threatened femininity of political whiteness. It hides the fact that many people facilitating others' sex work are sex workers themselves, and ignores the fact that sex workers have consistently resisted the inclusion of managers in their movement for labour rights.

'Pimp lobby' outrage means that when sex workers demand decriminalisation, their feminist opponents can dismiss them as 'happy hookers' who do not care about 'women's safety'. Even though, in the words of the English Collective of Prostitutes, sex workers want decriminalisation *for safety's sake*. As authors and sex workers Juno Mac and Molly Smith argue, the call to 'listen to survivors' means that the category of survivors who advocate for decriminalising sex work cannot, or should not, exist.[25] This is how anti-sex-industry feminism monopolises the right to protection, through claiming ownership of sexual trauma. This is how – despite its definition of sex work as 'paid rape' – it erases the sexual trauma of a particularly marginalised group of women. It prices sex workers out of the outrage market using the figure of the sex industry survivor.

In its use of sex industry survivors, this feminism also draws on the long tradition of colonial feminist 'empathy' for the Other. And this 'empathy' is actually a form of consumption.[26] We know it is self-serving, because the sex industry survivor is consumed to deflect opposition from another Other (the sex worker advocating for labour rights). The Other is spoken for, to defeat other Others who are speaking for themselves.

This is also carceral feminism – committed to using the criminal punishment system for social change. It reconciles punishment with 'empathy' through its view of the state as benign: interventions made into the sex industry protect non-sex-working women, and are for sex workers' 'own good'. Anti-sex-industry feminists do not reserve any outrage for sex workers subject to state violence. Women such as Yang Song, who in 2017 jumped to her death from a fourth-floor window to avoid arrest in a vice raid at the New York massage parlour where she worked. She had been arrested before; someone claiming to be a police officer had also assaulted her. Or Layleen Cubilette-Polanco, arrested in 2019 accused of biting a cab driver. Because of a previous arrest for prostitution and drugs offences, and because she did not attend all the classes mandated by the Manhattan human trafficking court's 'diversion program', Cubilette-Polanco's bail was set at $500. She couldn't pay it, and so was sent to Rikers Island, where she died less than two months later.

#SayHerName was launched in 2014 by the African American Policy Forum and Kimberlé Crenshaw's Center for Intersectionality and Social Policy Studies at Columbia. Originally started in response to Black Lives Matter as a way of highlighting Black women's experiences, it has now become a powerful movement lifting up the names of Black women subject to state violence.[27] Especially women who have lost their lives: women like Sandra Bland, Tanisha Anderson and Rekia Boyd. And women like Layleen Cubilette-Polanco.

But when stories such as Song's and Cubilette-Polanco's are reported, anti-sex-industry feminists do not say their names. Especially when the victim is a trans woman, as Cubilette-Polanco was, because anti-sex-industry and anti-trans feminism are inextricably linked. And like the sex industry debates, discussions of transgender inclusion – in spaces such as women's refuges, prisons, changing rooms and bathrooms – involve privileged feminists pricing others out of the outrage economy.

In trans-exclusionary feminism, the sexual traumas of cis women sit beside a construction of trans women as predatory, dangerous and essentially male. Julia Serano describes this with precision in her book *Excluded*. She recounts being interviewed by a graduate student visiting Camp Trans, the yearly event by trans women and allies protesting the Michigan Womyn's Music Festival's trans-exclusionary policy of 'womyn-only space'. It was only a matter of time, Serano writes, before the line of questioning arrived at the 'penis issue'. At this point, she recalls, the student's partner 'burst out with questions of her own'.

> While there were several of us being interviewed, she turned directly to me, and in a terse and condescending tone of voice, said: 'How dare you! You have no idea what many of these women have been through. Don't you understand that many of them are abuse survivors who could be triggered by you? Can't you see why some women might not feel safe having you and your penis around?'[28]

This outburst exemplifies how trans-exclusionary feminism uses the experience of rape. Drawing on the radical feminist idea of the penis as a weapon, it 'sticks' this organ to trans women through an obsession with their surgical status. The 'threat' posed by the trans woman is then juxtaposed with the threatened (white) femininity of the abuse survivor. Cue outrage.

In 2014 a group of feminists started the hashtag #NoUnexpectedPenises. This combined stories of sexual abuse with statements against trans-inclusion. One read: 'I've had men rub their erect penises against me on the tube ... but apparently if I say I don't want a penis around me I am a bigot. Fuck. That.' Another said: 'Do people really not see that telling lesbians "trans women are women" is promoting rape culture?' The phrase 'no unexpected penises' has become common in trans-exclusionary feminist discourse. It evokes an organ with a life of its own, which is threatening because it is hidden (maybe, like the stranger rapist, it might jump out from the darkness). It also roots sexual violence in biology, rather than understanding it as a product of intersecting power relations.

There is no convincing evidence that trans women are more likely to perpetrate sexual violence than cis women are. There is a much mis-cited Swedish cohort study from 2011, which found that trans women in the earlier part of the cohort had similar rates of crime convictions to cis men. However, these convictions were mainly for poverty-related crimes, and as social support increased throughout the study's thirty-year period, the conviction rates of trans women decreased.[29] Nevertheless, isolated incidents of trans women perpetrating sexual violence are invested in the outrage economy, to generate maximum emotion and construct all trans women as a threat.

An example: Karen White. White is a trans woman convicted of sex offences, who was transferred to a West Yorkshire women's prison in 2017 and sexually assaulted two other inmates there. This generated legitimate outrage. But much of this outrage was manipulated, by feminist groups and in the right-wing press, to create general opposition to trans equality. A petition by Fair Play for Women, signed by almost 11,000 people, called on the government to 'review rules that allow[ed] male prisoners who identify as female in women's prisons'. And the Ministry of Justice did this; it also moved several trans women into the male estate. In 2015 two trans women, Vicky Thompson and Joanne Latham, died by suicide in the space of two months while being held in male prisons in the UK. Two years later, in the Karen White case, a massive failure of risk assessment on the part of HM Prison Service was turned into an argument against trans rights.

Like other reactionary politics, trans-exclusionary feminism generates outrage through constructing all trans women as dangerous in response to isolated incidents. The effect of this is to repackage trans equality itself as predation: trans women's demands to be recognised *as women* are reinterpreted as invasion and sexual threat. Trans women seeking refuge and support, or just getting on with their lives (by using public changing rooms or bathrooms), are invested with malign and rapacious intent. And this has peaked in the reaction to the term 'cotton ceiling', used to describe the dating and sexual barriers that queer trans women face. The term is certainly problematic: it evokes the 'glass ceiling' of barriers against the career progression that women are *entitled to*, compared to men with similar qualifications and skills. But as philosopher Amia Srinivasan has said, it expresses a valid point. Desire is socially constructed – and trans bodies, along with those of people marginalised by other categories such as race, disability and age, are often seen as undesirable and ruled out on spec.[30]

This means that examining desire critically is necessary – which does not mean that people who do not want to have sex with us, should. But in response to ideas about the 'cotton ceiling', trans-exclusionary feminists have compared trans women to incels and accused them of violent sexual entitlement. Discussions about disgust directed at trans bodies, or the right time in a relationship to reveal one's trans status, have been represented as 'sex by stealth' or 'corrective rape' on lesbians. In 2019 the feminist group OBJECT! claimed:

> The 'trans' phenomenon has allowed homophobic 'grooming' of lesbians (conversion therapy) to go unde-tected. The psychological manipulation of lesbians to accept men as sexual partners occurs within 'LGBT'

spaces, both online and offline. The rallying cry of 'trans' ideology, 'TRANSWOMEN ARE WOMEN', means that a man can be a lesbian. This is inherently misogynistic and lesbophobic. We OBJECT. Only women can be lesbians.[31]

This idea of the trans woman as predator is powerful in a world where transphobia is virulent and on the rise. It has been picked up on the right, where it is central to trans-exclusionary 'bathroom bills', or ordinances against trans-inclusive ones, proposed in many US states. During Obama's presidency, the US Departments of Justice and Education issued guidance to public schools advising them, among other things, to allow trans students to use the bathroom that best matched their gender. In response, James Dobson (who helped found the anti-LGBTQ organisations Focus on the Family and the Family Research Council) wrote: 'If you are a dad, I pray you will protect your little girls from men who walk in unannounced, unzip their pants and urinate in front of them. If this had happened 100 years ago, someone might have been shot. Where is today's manhood? God help us!'[32]

Also in 2016, and in response to a trans-inclusive bathroom bill, North Carolina Governor Pat McCrory warned citizens of the dangers of letting people with 'male anatomy' into female space.[33] In 2017 a letter signed by more than 750 ministers supporting a trans-exclusionary bathroom bill in Texas read: 'the privacy, safety and freedom of our women and children are not for sale at any price'.[34]

In both right-wing and trans-exclusionary feminist circles, outrage is generated by investing experiences of and fears about rape. And like the discussions
around sex work, this is also a claim to ownership of
sexual trauma, this time on behalf of cis women. This
hides the fact that trans people are particularly vulnerable to sexual victimisation. The 2015 US Transgender
Survey found that 47 per cent of trans people are sexually assaulted at some point in their lifetime.[35] But we
are asked to ignore statistics such as this and 'listen to
survivors': those who fear trans women's inclusion in
women-only space. The designation 'survivor', and its
claim on our empathy and outrage, is withheld from
trans women. Like sex workers, they are priced out of
the outrage economy (and a significant number of trans
women are sex workers as well).

The investment of sexual trauma in the outrage
economy allows the 'good' woman (cis, 'respectable',
implicitly white) to be used to withhold support and
resources from the 'bad' ones. Trans women and sex
workers are pitted against more privileged women, in a
politics that does not challenge how neoliberal capitalism has created massive inequalities of distribution.
This politics does not focus on safer workplaces for all
and better-funded women's services. It is not centred
on opposing the austerity budgets that have pushed
many women into selling sex. Instead, it positions
trans women and 'happy hookers' as the enemy.

This politics also *creates* risks of violence: for
instance, for sex workers dealing with the effects of

criminalisation, and trans women made to use men's bathrooms or incarcerated in men's prisons. Melissa Gira Grant has called this feminism's own 'war on women', where some women are subjected to poverty, violence and prison in the name of defending other women's rights.[36] In the next two chapters, I will examine this 'war machine' of white feminism in more detail.

## Chapter 5

# White feminism as war machine

On 21 January 2017 more than 5 million women and people of other genders took to the streets in US cities. It was the day after President Trump's inauguration. His candidacy for the presidency had put sexism and sexual violence centre stage, prompting seventeen allegations of harassment and/or assault. These arose after the leak of a 2005 recording in which Trump bragged about being able to 'do anything' to women. 'When you're a star', he said, 'they let you do it. You can do anything. Grab 'em by the pussy.'

One of the most talked-about banners of the 2017 Women's March said: 'Pussy Grabs Back.' Other slogans included 'Stop Fucking with Us', 'Dump Trump' and 'Women Roar'. Some protestors dressed as witches; a corresponding placard said: 'We are the granddaughters of the witches you weren't able to burn.' Similar marches occurred in 84 other countries, one of the largest public protests by women in history. Also known as: collective rage. Rebecca Traister called the march a 'cascade of wrath'.[1] Columnist Michelle Goldberg declared that 'the Trump resistance [would] be led by angry women'.[2] This was partly based on a nationally representative survey conducted in 2016 by PerryUndem, which found that anger over Trump's sexism had done more than anything else to spur people to political action.

To understand the Women's March, Goldberg explained, one had to understand 'just how devastated, shocked, and even traumatized many women [were] by the election of the grab-'em-by-the-pussy president'. The march, followed by the viral spread of #MeToo later that year, led to 2017 being characterised as 'the year of women's anger'. It was a year – *the* year – in which women finally let it out. Writing in *Vox*, Constance Grady said:

> And so the year that began with the Women's March, in which millions of pussy-hatted women came together to protest the Trump administration, ended with the Reckoning, in which hundreds of women have come forward to accuse powerful men of acts of sexual violence, and dozens of those men have been fired or resigned in disgrace. And in between, popular culture has told story after story about angry women who are burning shit down.[3]

'Yes, this is a witch hunt', wrote author and comedian Lindy West in the *New York Times*. 'I'm a witch and I'm hunting you.'[4] To borrow a phrase from Sara Ahmed, this outpouring of anger could be seen as a moment of 'feminist snap'. We snap, suggests Ahmed, when we are fed up with negotiating worlds that demean and exclude us. For Ahmed, snapping is both expressive and potentially transformative – she calls feminist history a 'history of snappy women'.[5] Both the Women's March and #MeToo are forms of what Ahmed calls 'collective snap', outpourings from women and people of other genders who came together in common anger and resistance.

The year of women's anger punctuated what essayist Pankaj Mishra calls the 'age of anger', marked by economic shocks, information and culture wars, terrorism and state response, and framed by the rhetoric of a 'clash of civilisations' between Islam and the West. Mishra argues that as globalisation and financial crisis have weakened older forms of authority, and as welfare states and community structures have declined, people increasingly feel that 'there is no such thing as society or state, and that there is only a war of all against all'.[6] This anger is sometimes expressed as outrage in the economies of networked and social media. It is sometimes expressed at the ballot box. And sometimes it takes us to the streets.

Anger drives many contemporary progressive movements, on issues such as austerity, borders, climate change and sexual violence. It also powers the global swing to the right. Our right-moving world centres the anger of those who have lost privileges and entitlements, or who feel 'left behind' and are blaming the wrong people. This is the anger of white men, and some white women too. Far-right politics shows us what happens when anger is produced by – and channelled through – class and race supremacy.

And this is also relevant to white women's anger about sexual violence. Public expressions of feminist anger, such as the Women's March, are undeniably bourgeois and white. So are the majority of feminist investments in the outrage economy of the media. Bourgeois white women, like all women, have a right to be angry about sexual violence. But this anger is shaped by our race and class positions. This raises a number of questions: how is mainstream feminist anger generated, how does it express itself, and what, ultimately, does it do?

## The (mis)uses of anger

'This is a book for women who know shit is fucked up', wrote Brittney Cooper on the first page of her 2018 book *Eloquent Rage: A Black Feminist Discovers her Superpower*. *Eloquent Rage* was the first of several popular feminist books on women's anger published in the wake of the Women's March and #MeToo. Soraya Chemaly's *Rage Becomes Her: The Power of Women's Anger* and Rebecca Traister's *Good and Mad: The Revolutionary Power of Women's Anger* were both released later in 2018.

All three books equated women's anger with power. Cooper's was written from her perspective as a Black woman, focused on her own struggle to embrace anger in the face of white supremacist dismissal and Black respectability politics. Chemaly's also focused on how women could embrace their anger to create positive change, calling it a 'walking talking refutation of [the] status quo'.[7] Traister's explored how the impulse to be 'really mad' had been long suppressed in women, but was crucial to their political power and social standing. This equation of anger with power has a long and useful history in feminism.

In Black feminist traditions especially, drawing from Black radicalism, anger and violent resistance are seen as ways to counter the devaluation of Black lives. As organiser, writer, researcher and educator Mariame Kaba has said: 'to insist that you deserve to live, by any means necessary, is an act of radical self-love'.[8] Anger is a way of reclaiming the self, a way to avoid internalising oppression, and a way to fight back. It is an emotional and political defence system. In Audre Lorde's influential essay 'The Uses of Anger', she writes that every woman has a 'well-stocked arsenal of anger potentially useful against those oppressions, personal and institutional, which brought that anger into being'.[9]

Feminist anger is powerful because power demands submission. And as Sara Ahmed writes, this demand means that those in power can dismiss others' expressions of will as 'willful'. This is exemplified in the familiar figure of the 'wilful child'. It also creates the figure of the 'feminist killjoy', who rejects the silence and compliance of femininity and in the process *ruins everything*. Feminist killjoys fume when they should smile – philosopher Alison Jaggar calls feminist anger an 'outlaw emotion', because it breaks with gendered convention.[10] For Ahmed, feminist, queer and anti-racist movements are performances of willfulness, questioning authority and debating sovereignty, and embracing and subverting identity-based stigma.[11]

Feminist killjoys and emotional outlaws are unwilling to be 'nice'. This is a politics of refusal. It refuses the demands for 'kindness' and 'civility' imposed by those in power upon the powerless. In the process, it exposes how these demands are gendered, classed and raced. Heteropatriarchy demands that women not only serve, but also love, their oppressors. Neoliberal capitalism demands emotional labour: we are not only required to graft, but to love our work (and show it).[12] And the conqueror, settler and master demand willing, and absolute, subjugation. The psychological violence of colonialism was embodied in the figure of the 'happy slave': colonised and enslaved people were expected to perform acceptance of, and even contentment with, their own oppression (although many did not).[13]

Demands for civility also loom large in our current political landscape. On the right, feminists and other social justice activists are monstered as censorial and oppressive, because we name and resist oppression. And from liberals, the demand to be 'nice' is couched in the language of 'free speech' and 'balanced debate'. This is based in the conviction that reasonable debate can counter and even defeat unreasonable and dangerous ideas. And as Anderson and Samudzi argue, it betrays the belief that 'one side's dehumanization of another is just a difference of opinion'.[14]

Civility is white supremacy. And the demand that marginalised people perform civility while being dehumanised produces what Cooper calls the 'rage management project' of respectability politics.[15] This is the injunction from *within* marginalised communities that we don't get too angry, don't behave badly and don't rock the boat. It is a survival strategy, particularly for Black people in the face of privileged white communities' and states' capacities for violence.

'Respectability' is also a central characteristic of bourgeois white femininity. And unlike their fore-mothers, today's white feminists often push against it: see 'Pussy Grabs Back', the Women's Marchers dressed as witches, and the self-identified 'nasty women' who populate our contemporary feminist landscape. The phrase 'nasty woman' became a feminist rally-ing cry during Hillary Clinton's campaign for the US presidency, after Trump used it about her in the final debate. Being 'nasty' is a way to kick back against the patriarchal demand that women always be nice.

However, claiming the right to be nasty in resist-ance to gendered respectability politics is often done by women who continue to be positioned as respect-able by the world at large. And the 'respectability' of bourgeois white women has been central to colonial narratives that construct us as superior to women mar-ginalised by race and class. Affronts to this 'respectabil-ity' have justified fatal violence against men of colour. This position of race and class supremacy means that our anger may not always be as radical or transgressive as we might like. This chapter asks: what happens to willfulness, when it is channelled through whiteness? As Ahmed argues, sometimes what is thought or said to be willfulness can instead be willing whiteness – which maintains, rather than challenging, the status quo.[16] I want to develop this point.

## Whose anger is it anyway? (or Me, Not You)

One of the things white feminist anger does is sideline or dismiss the anger of women of colour. Black feminists especially have made huge contributions to theorising and politicising anger. But in mainstream feminism, their emotions have not been the priority. Audre Lorde's famous essay on anger highlights how white women's anger is too often misdirected at Black women who highlight racism, rather than at the powers-that-be. The 'angry Black woman' is 'too angry' for white men and women alike. This is political whiteness at work, shaped by colonial ideas about the 'savagery' of Black people and other people of colour.

Although the 2017 Women's March was co-led by three women of colour (Tamika Mallory, Carmen Perez and Linda Sarsour, alongside Bob Bland), and although its speakers included Angela Davis and authors Raquel Willis and Janet Mock (both of whom are Black trans women), it was criticised for centring privileged white women. In her speech, Willis said: 'although I'm glad to be here now, it's disheartening that women like me were an afterthought'. Women of colour who

attended the Washington march reported being disre-
spected, dismissed and fetishised by the white women
marching beside them.[17] On Twitter, Mvskoke feminist Sydne Gray (@sydnerain) said that although white
women took pictures of her prayer circle, they refused
to accept flyers on pipelines, fracking and missing
and murdered Indigenous women. She also said that
Native American women were scolded for being 'too
loud'. This is a familiar dynamic – while bourgeois
white women claim our right to be 'nasty', we expect
more marginalised women to be nice.

The Women's March was also beset by allegations of
antisemitism and critiqued for removing a statement
of solidarity with sex workers from its website. The
pink pussy hats worn by some marchers were seen as
white- and cis-centric. The original event was called
the 'Million Women March', until it was pointed out
on social media that Black women had held a demonstration with this title in 1997, partly in response to
their lack of representation in the mainstream feminist movement.[18] And as always, such calls to address
white privilege were met by white feminist calls for
'unity' – 'niceness' in another guise.

The Women's March is a recent instalment in the
history of public feminist rage, which also includes
the suffrage marches, the civil disobedience of the
suffragettes and the many speak-outs and protests of
Women's Liberation. This history is deeply inflected
by whiteness. In 1913 the organisers of a large suffragist parade in Washington demanded that Black

participants march at the back, instead of with their state delegations. Ida B. Wells famously refused.[19] Second-wave protests such as Reclaim the Night contained relatively few Black women (perhaps unsurprising given their links with state and vigilante policing of the streets).

The Slutwalks of the early 2010s are also part of this history. Social scientists Jessica Ringrose and Emma Renold, drawing on the theories of Deleuze and Guattari, have called Slutwalk a 'war machine'.[20] It was a powerful rejection of respectability: women claimed their right to dress and behave in sexual ways, without risk of sexual violence. But there were discussions at the time about whose tactics these were. In 2011 Black Women's Blueprint wrote an open letter to the Slutwalk, which said:

> As Black women, we do not have the privilege or the space to call ourselves 'slut' without validating the already historically entrenched ideology and recurring messages about what and who the Black woman is. We don't have the privilege to play on destructive representations burned in our collective minds, on our bodies and souls for generations.[21]

While white women rejected respectability politics and claimed our right to be 'sluts', Black women could not adopt this strategy because of the colonial history of violent sexualisation of Black bodies. The open letter to the Slutwalk also said this strategy could *create* increased discrimination and violence. This is the collateral damage of the white feminist war machine.

Racialised dynamics like this are hidden by the general category of 'women's rage'. It trains our sights on gender, and away from race and class. It positions bourgeois white women as victims, and erases our complicity in racial capitalist exploitation and white supremacy. Let's go back to 'nasty woman' Hillary Clinton. Clinton supported (among other things) the 1994 Crime Bill and welfare reform legislation that disproportionately targeted Black people. She referred to Black kids as 'superpredators' in a 1996 speech defending that legislation.[22] As Obama's Secretary of State she was known for her hawkish foreign policy, which embraced using deadly military power against populations in the service of US political and economic interests. Hillary Clinton has also been a victim of gross sexism. But reclaiming her right to be 'nasty' as part of an anti-patriarchal project whitewashes those (truly nasty) acts right out of the picture.

The category of 'women's rage' hides the fact that white women's anger can be associated with deeply reactionary politics. As Cooper writes, the rage of white supremacist men leads to fascism through fears that white power might be slipping away.[23] But white women were also part of the angry reaction that produced Brexit, Trump and the elevation of far-right figures and parties worldwide. According to exit polls, 53 per cent of white women voted for Trump, compared to 94 per cent of Black women who voted for Clinton (despite their reservations). And as Jessie Daniels reminds us, the majority of white women in the US have voted Republican for decades – 90 per cent of white women are married to white men, with a major stake in their economic power.[24] A number of white women have made names for themselves as leaders of the resurgent far right: Marine Le Pen of France's Front National, Alice Weidel of the German AfD and Giorgia Meloni of the Brothers of Italy, to name a few. Their white rage is white power, yet many white feminists celebrate 'women's rage' as if it is always a feminist emotion.

Cooper did not go to the Women's March because of the role of white women in electing Trump. Watching white women protest the election, she wrote, when 'white women's powerful voting bloc' was partly responsible for it, felt like 'an exercise in white-lady tears if I ever saw one'.[25] White women's tears are a way of maintaining white innocence, a way of pointing the finger away from us and at someone else.[26] White women's anger can be, too. Read through this lens, the Women's March could be seen as an exercise that hid white women's complicity in the election of Trump, and in white supremacy in general, under a cloak of feminist rage.

## White feminism as war machine

*The Hound. Meryn Trant. Joffrey. The Red Woman. Thoros. Cersei. Ilyn Payne. Polliver. The Mountain. Rorge. Walder Frey. Tywin Lannister. Beric Dondarrion.*

This is Arya Stark's 'kill list' from the TV phenomenon *Game of Thrones*. Early in the series, the young Arya began reciting the names of those who had wronged her. And many of them ended up dead, at the point of Arya's sword or those of others (in one particularly gruesome scene she kills Walder Frey's sons and bakes them into a pie, which she serves to him before cutting his throat). Arya is a traumatised and brutalised figure. She sees her father publicly beheaded. She is separated from the rest of her family and then discovers that most of them have been killed. She experiences home-lessness, physical violence, and constant threats of rape and death. Her journey is one of empowerment through anger and vigilante justice; she is the opposite of 'respectable' femininity. As Shahida Arabi has writ-ten in *Bitch* magazine:

> Unlike a woman who turns the other cheek and goes immediately into love and light without any kind of transformation beforehand, Arya turns to her sword, Needle, to deliver a much-needed message to perpe-trators. The North remembers, and so does she. She avenges her loved ones one by one, and when she does, we can't help but cheer from the sidelines.[27]

There was debate about the gender politics of *Game of Thrones*, mainly focused on its frequent and often gratuitous depictions of sexual violence. But Arya and her sister Sansa, as well as the 'mother of dragons' Daenerys Targaryen, were seen by some as feminist heroes. Sansa gets revenge by leaving her rapist Ramsay Bolton to be eaten by his own dogs. Daenerys becomes the show's white saviour queen, using deadly violence to liberate an amorphous mass of characters of colour from slavery (and eventually turning to indiscriminate slaughter when her power is threatened).

*Game of Thrones* is a paradigm artefact for the contemporary 'age of anger'. It represents the war of all against all – it is dark and nihilistic. Most characters are motivated by power and revenge, rather than the greater good. The show eroticises punishment and violence: its key themes are sex, dominance and death, and it harks back to the public passion for blood that characterised the ancient world. For Arabi, Arya Stark also embodies the revenge fantasies that all survivors have. She is 'is every little girl who grew up in terror and trauma … She is all of us who have survived – and thrived.' And like most of the other main characters in the series, Arya is also white.

*Harvey Weinstein. Larry Nassar. Kevin Spacey. Junot Diaz. Richard Dreyfuss. Gerard Depardieu. James Franco. David Copperfield. Sylvester Stallone. The 'shitty media men'.*

This is part of the 'kill list' of #MeToo. 'Naming and shaming' these men and others in the media outrage economy was a key tactic of the movement. These men were not mortally wounded, although the backlash claimed that they were – many managed to evade any consequences at all. Naming and shaming them was intended to create accountability through exposure, triggering organisational and institutional discipline, and/or criminal punishment. Interviewed by Hari Sreenivasan on *PBS Newshour* in November 2017, Tarana Burke reflected on these tactics. 'Every day there's a new person that comes out', she said, 'and everybody has shock and awe.' I want to explore the 'shock and awe' of the white feminist 'war machine' in more detail.

In his famous article 'Necropolitics', political theorist Achille Mbembe uses the idea of the 'war machine' to characterise contemporary militias, both state-allied and opposed, which aim to force the enemy into submission regardless of the cost or collateral damage. For Mbembe, contemporary political sovereignty is *necropolitical*: literally the power to decide who will live and who will die.[28] Sometimes this is accomplished actively, through a military invasion or incursion. Sometimes it is done through fatal neglect of populations deemed surplus to capitalist production: people living in slums, or displaced migrants interned in camps or, alternatively, left to drown. The *necropolis* is populated by these 'outsiders', as well as the hyperexploited populations of colour who prop up capitalism from the margins but are treated as expendable. And this polis is also expendable, treated as collateral, in the strategies and tactics of mainstream feminism.

The feminist 'war machine' is white. And white rage is necropolitical rage: political whiteness is characterised by a desire for power and punishment. When righteous anger about sexual violence is channelled

through race and class supremacy, it can produce a
need for *infliction*. Outside fictional representations
such as *Game of Thrones*, this is not usually the infliction of physical death. But it can be the social death of
incarceration: a loss of humanity, neglect and reduc-
tion to what philosopher Giorgio Agamben calls 'bare
life'.[29] It is mostly people of colour who may already be
living 'bare' lives (and especially Black people whose
lives are marked by histories of slavery and segregation) that are 'put away' by the criminal punishment
system. This system is designed to contain and disen-
franchise communities that are already unemployed,
underemployed or precariously employed, existing
in the necropolis. According to the NAACP, African
American people are incarcerated at more than five
times the rate of whites.[30]

In 2019 Ava DuVernay's acclaimed Netflix series
*When They See Us* dramatised the story of the
Exonerated Five (previously known as the Central Park
Five). The Five – all African American or Latinx men –
are Antron McCray, Kevin Richardson, Yusef Salaam,
Raymond Santana and Korey Wise. All were teenagers when they were wrongly convicted of the violent
sexual assault of Trisha Meili (the Central Park Jogger)
in 1989. They all served sentences of between six and
thirteen years. Overseeing the prosecution was Linda
Fairstein, a white woman and hero of carceral feminism who saw herself as a crusader against sexual violence and prostitution. Kelly McGillis had consulted
Fairstein to prepare for her role as the prosecutor in the

1988 film *The Accused*. On 25 February 1990 a celebratory profile in the *New York Times* was entitled 'Linda Fairstein vs. Rape'.

*When They See Us* portrays the intense media outrage that accompanied the Exonerated Five case, focused on young Black men 'wilding' on the streets of New York. It depicts Fairstein as pursuing conviction at any price: overseeing coerced confessions, dismissing the doubts of law enforcement, and ignoring evidence that pointed to the boys' innocence. In 2002 the Five's convictions were all struck down after Matias Reyes, already convicted of serial rape and murder, confessed to being the sole perpetrator of the crime (confirmed by DNA testing). But Fairstein maintained that they were guilty. In July 2018 she wrote a letter to the *New York Law Journal* entitled 'In Defense of the Central Park 5 Prosecution'.

The injustices wreaked on the Exonerated Five were collateral damage of Linda Fairstein's carceral feminist crusade, itself a tool of a criminal punishment system designed to control people marginalised by race and class. And in 2017 it was reported that Fairstein had been involved in *quashing* allegations against Harvey Weinstein made by Filipina-Italian model Ambra Battilana (now Ambra Gutierrez) in 2015. Alongside a counterattack involving private investigators and leaks designed to discredit Battilana in the press, Fairstein had facilitated the introduction of Weinstein's attorneys to the sex crimes prosecutor handling the case.[31] Fairstein, it seems, believes that accountability should be selective. In contrast, carceral feminism in #MeToo and similar movements generally does not – but it legitimises the criminal punishment system by arguing that privileged white men should not be exempt from social death.

Of course, #MeToo and similar movements do not always demand incarceration. In 2017 columnist Moira Donegan put the 'shitty media men' spreadsheet on Google, which collated rumours and warnings about sexual abuse. Independently but at the same time, law student and queer Dalit feminist Raya Sarkar put a similar list of Indian academics on Facebook. Both lists were warnings to women in the respective industries, and put current and potential employers on notice. And unlike the social death of the prison, losing one's job seems a fair consequence for perpetrating abuse. Abusers do not have a right to high-status and lucrative employment, or to membership of particular professions or communities. Refusing to exclude abusers is a de facto exclusion of survivors. But as I argued in the previous chapter, excluding perpetrators may be more like NIMBYism than radical politics. Like capitalism itself, this moves problems around rather than addressing them; ultimately, we may outsource our harassers to women in lower-status, lower-paid economic sectors. Like the Black women who wrote to the Slutwalk, women in the global proletariat (many of whom are women of colour) can become collateral damage of the white feminist 'war machine'.[32]

The infliction that comes with white feminist anger, with its willingness to create collateral damage, perhaps makes it less of an 'outlaw' emotion than we might wish. In the symbolic and material game of 'cops and robbers', we are often identified with the cops. As Angela Davis has said: 'we often do the work of the state in and through our interior lives'.[33] This pertains particularly to white women, and perhaps especially those of us in anti-rape movements. Our anger at heteropatriarchy demands criminal and institutional punishment. But saying 'fuck the patriarchy' is hardly radical when this is followed by calling on patriarchal disciplinary power.

This differentiates white feminism from both the Black radical and anti-fascist traditions of protest, which mobilise *against* the state. 'Antifa' are often defined as 'violent' because they are not afraid to get physical, to punch a Nazi (or sometimes to throw a milkshake at one). But to borrow journalist and scholar Natasha Lennard's analysis, these are *counter-violences* aimed at disrupting violent ideologies and forms of power.[34] In contrast, protests such as the Women's March (and other white-dominated movements such as Extinction Rebellion) tend to pride themselves on their 'non-violence', while legitimating and even calling on the power that anti-fascists resist. With police indulgently looking on, bourgeois white women demand state intervention to get the 'bad men' (regardless of the fact that sexual violence and abuse are perpetrated by law enforcement officers in significant numbers).

The Women's March was focused on Trump – the biggest, baddest 'bad man' of all. But it did not extend to critique of the systems that produced him. It can be contrasted with the Women's Strike, a far less high-profile movement that is intersectional, anti-capitalist, international and focused on the 'red feminist horizon'. The difference between the two is the difference between politics focused on interpersonal power and politics focused on structural oppression. And the qualities of mainstream feminist anger complicate our claims to willfulness, which for Ahmed is a way of questioning authority and sovereignty. Although mainstream feminist activism is willful in its defiance of gender inequality, its solutions tend to revert to the status quo.

## Will or be willed, kill or be killed

In Chapter 3 I argued that the will to power of political whiteness might be intensified by the need for power and control produced by sexual trauma. As Ahmed reminds us, Susan Brownmiller's famous book on rape is called *Against Our Will*.[35] Violations of will may produce a need to be 'willful' – I have felt that need myself. But when filtered through race and class supremacy, the willfulness that follows violation may create a deep need for our will to be done. I fear that the white feminist focus on infliction may be an example of what Lennard calls 'fascistic habit'.[36] This is the love of power and authority, and desire to dominate, oppress and obliterate the Other, that exists in all of us. That it is largely turned on white and privileged men does not make the desire any less problematic, or the systems we use to fulfil it any more humane.

In *Game of Thrones*, you win or you die. This scenario of 'kill or be killed' is classic necropolitics. To go back to Mbembe:

> The survivor is the one who, having stood in the path of death, knowing of many deaths and standing in the midst of the fallen, is still alive. Or, more precisely, the survivor is the one who has taken on a whole pack of enemies and managed not only to escape alive, but to kill his or her attackers. This is why, to a large extent, the lowest form of survival is killing.[37]

At a very basic level, anti-rape activism is about survival. Many of us are survivors trying to survive, and spectacles of mass wounding such as #MeToo evoke a gendered state of siege. Being raped often involves a visceral fear of death, whether the rape is physically violent or not – it is what makes us freeze, instead of fighting back. And if we freeze, perhaps we need our 'kill' after the experience is over. Unlike Arya Stark, we do not do our own killing. Instead, we ask the 'Angry Dad' or 'White Knight' of the state or institution to do it for us. And the destruction of bodily boundaries involved in criminal punishment mirrors the experience of rape.

Killing to protect white women has always been central to the necropolitics of race and imperialism. White supremacy is a politics of death: colonial massacres, lynchings, concentration camps. It constructs the Other as a mortal threat – often sexualised – which must be annihilated. White men protecting women from brown and Black men has justified many of these orgies of killing, from the genocide of Indigenous peoples to the bombs of the War on Terror. And white women are now represented at the highest levels of the neo-colonial war machine. As of January 2019, the CEOs of four of the five biggest US defence contractors – Northrop Grumman, Lockheed Martin, General Dynamics and the defence arm of Boeing – were white women. White women also held several of the Pentagon's top posts.[38] This war machine has dealt death and rape to people of colour on a massive scale.

'Kill or be killed' is the central message of the War on Terror, the 'monster hunt' which is part of the backdrop to contemporary feminism. Some of today's best-known feminist activists are well under 40, so may not remember a time without it. Lauren Berlant describes the War on Terror as the first 'war on an emotion', and with the aid of networked media it has put white fear centre stage.[39] It has produced and legitimated increased authoritarianism and carcerality under the banner of 'shock and awe'. It has shifted Western public consciousness in a more adversarial and threatened direction (and I say this as someone who grew up during the Cold War). Many mainstream feminists opposed, and continue to oppose, the War on Terror (although some colonial feminists have supported it). Regardless, this necropolitical consciousness cannot have failed to shape the white feminist war machine.

In colonial and settler-colonial cultures, as Cooper reminds us, white women's bodies are associated with freedom and Black women's with servitude.[40] In *Game of Thrones*, the only Black woman among the main characters is Missandei, who is emancipated from slavery. After she is freed by Daenerys she becomes the queen's advisor, until she is captured and beheaded in the final season. Beginning her journey in chains, this is also where Missandei ends it. She represents servitude while Arya Stark represents freedom. But freedom to do what? If sovereignty is necropolitical – deciding who is to live and who is to die – then Arya Stark achieves it.

Arya, along with the other white female principals of *Game of Thrones*, represents what Arruzza, Bhattacharya and Fraser might call 'equal opportunity domination'. This is the desire for individual power that leads to feminism being reduced to women busting unions, ordering drone strikes and locking children in cages.[41] This is the feminism that sees more female prison guards, more female soldiers, more female defence CEOs and ultimately a female Commander-in-Chief as social and political progress. Gender relations are currently being challenged and rethought, and equality gains staunchly defended as the resurgent right tries to roll them back. Perhaps this has given privileged white women the opportunity – and drive – to seize some power for ourselves. In a world of kill or be killed, or grab or be grabbed, this is *Pussy Grabs Back.*

I am aware that I am now travelling perilously close to the anti-feminist backlash. This presents stories of female anger alongside stories of male vulnerability to argue that men are now oppressed and subjugated. You may think I am asking: what about the men? You may wonder why women should not aspire to power, or seize it for ourselves. You may think I am asking women to shut up and be nice. As a white woman, sometimes I wonder if this *is* what I am unconsciously doing: in the absence of much power of its own, white womanhood tends to default to placating powerful white men.

But there are important and urgent questions here, which do not concern the powerful but come from the margins (where our focus should always be). White women have a right to be angry about sexual violence. Survivors have a right to spaces without abusers. All survivors fantasise about revenge. But whose bodies are forfeit when white women mobilise punitive state and institutional power to achieve it? Who are the real casualties of the white feminist war machine? In the final chapter I will approach these questions from another angle, and explore how some marginalised women have become enemies and not allies of this movement. This is where the 'Me, Not You' of white feminism ends up.

## Chapter 6

# Feminists and the far right

The 'fascistic habit' of white feminism can easily move from latent to overt. It is a short step from seeing more marginalised people as collateral, to positioning them as enemies when they thwart our will to power. Sara Ahmed has described how some feminists use 'willfulness' to support trans-exclusionary politics. They employ the figure of the 'feminist killjoy' to create the impression that trans-exclusionary feminism is a brave struggle against an oppressive majority. This is described as 'willful feminism', Ahmed writes, when it is in fact 'willing transphobia'.[1] Similar strategies underpin feminist campaigns against the sex industry, which set themselves against the fictional 'pimp lobby'. It is not surprising that the majority of trans-exclusionary and anti-sex-work feminists are white.

This reactionary feminism accelerates the white feminist 'war machine', using the media and social media outrage economy to maximum effect. Although its numbers are small, this movement is tightly networked and highly organised. Its tactics are similar to the notorious harassment campaign Gamergate:

it identifies and then relentlessly attacks target after target, seemingly with the aim of total submission. In Chapter 4 I described one of these attacks, against Amnesty International following its support for sex work decriminalisation. Prominent trans people (usually trans women) and trans-focused or trans-supportive organisations are also targeted, with increasing frequency.

In 2018 trans-exclusionary feminists mobilised against the UK Labour Party, after it clarified that its women-only shortlists were open to trans women. As a result, more than three hundred women resigned from the party in protest. Also in 2018 an open letter was circulated to Stonewall, attacking the organisation for supporting proposed changes to the 2004 UK Gender Recognition Act that would make it easier to change legal gender. At the same time, Stonewall and other international LGBT+ organisations were targeted by the #GettheLOut social media campaign. The hashtag had been used extensively after trans-exclusionary feminists disrupted London Pride, claiming that 'transactivism erase[d] lesbians'. The demand of #GettheLOut was that Stonewall and other organisations such as GLAAD, Lambda Legal, the Advocate and the Human Rights Campaign remove the 'L' from the acronym 'LGBT' in their mission statements. This was made after the organisations ignored a petition asking them to stop representing trans people.

After the UK Big Lottery fund awarded a grant of £500,000 to Mermaids, a charity supporting trans children and their families, it was subject to a campaign of letter-writing and social media messaging by trans-exclusionary feminists. Comedy writer Graham Linehan started the campaign on the online parenting forum Mumsnet, and it succeeded in convincing the Big Lottery fund to put the grant under review.[2] In response, gamer Harris Brewis (Hbomberguy) raised over £250,000 for Mermaids by playing *Donkey Kong* for more than two days. His Twitch stream during the marathon featured guests including Alexandria Ocasio-Cortez and Chelsea Manning. In retaliation, an 83-page thread was generated about Brewis on the far-right stalking and harassment forum Kiwi Farms, claiming that he had raised money for a 'child abuse cult'. The Big Lottery grant to Mermaids was eventually confirmed.

Writing in *Vogue* after the Mermaids furore had died down, Paris Lees said: 'God knows what lack of humanity possesses people to target vulnerable children and their families.'[3] This lack of humanity is political whiteness – the thicker end of the wedge. Trans-exclusionary and anti-sex-work feminism amplify the mainstream movement's desire for power and authority, and pursue it by policing the borders of feminism and womanhood. The mainstream preoccupation with threat becomes an overt 'us and them' mentality, and the necropolitical desire for annihilation is deliberately turned on more marginalised people.

## (Un)holy alliances

Unsurprisingly, reactionary feminists have often found allies on the right. In 2018 religious conservatives and feminists jointly backed the Stop Enabling Sex Traffickers Act (SESTA) and the Allow States and Victims to Fight Online Sex Trafficking Act (FOSTA) in the US. The Acts banned online advertising of sexual services, also potentially preventing sex workers from using the Internet to organise, share safety information and screen potential clients. Advocates of SESTA/FOSTA, including Senator Kamala Harris, gave support over the objections of many trafficking survivors and their allies. The key objection was that by stopping sex workers from working on their own terms, the Acts would increase vulnerability to exploitation, especially for migrant and/or low-income sex workers, sex workers of colour and/or trans sex workers, who would be forced to choose between safety and survival.

The synergy between feminists and the religious right on sex work is perhaps best remembered from the anti-porn campaigns of the 1980s. 'When Jerry Falwell starts saying there's real harm in pornography, then that is valuable to me', Andrea Dworkin commented in 1985. A few years earlier, trans-exclusionary feminist Janice Raymond – author of the notorious *The Transsexual Empire* – had written a paper for the Reagan administration which guided its 1981 decision to deny Medicare for sex-reassignment surgery. In the 1990s Raymond turned her attention from transgender issues to sex trafficking – like many trans-exclusionary feminists, she is anti sex worker as well. The connection between the two ideologies peaks in scornful descriptions of trans women as 'pornified' representations of femininity rather than 'real women' (implying that sex workers are not 'real women' either).

Recently the right-wing connections of trans-exclusionary feminists have been boosted, because of broader rightward shifts that have involved increasingly open hostility to trans people. This has created a situation in which material alliances can be made. Hands Across the Aisle, co-founded by anti-abortion activist Kaeley Triller, is an initiative that aims to unite right-wing organisations with trans-exclusionary feminists and groups. Through Hands Across the Aisle, feminists associate with the US National Catholic Bioethics Center, the American College of Pediatricians (an anti-LGBT group not to be confused with the American Academy of Pediatrics) and Tucker Carlson's website the Daily Caller (which has published pieces by white supremacists and neo-Nazis).[4] Hands Across the Aisle's mission statement reads: 'We are radical feminists, lesbians, Christians and conservatives that are tabling our ideological differences to stand in solidarity against gender identity legislation, which we have come to recognize as the erasure of our own hard-won civil rights.'

One of the feminist groups associated with Hands Across the Aisle is the US-based Women's Liberation Front (WoLF), founded in 2014 to 'end male violence, regain reproductive sovereignty, and ultimately dismantle the gender-caste system'. In reality, the group appears to restrict itself mainly to trans-exclusionary campaigning. In 2018 its representative Julia Beck appeared on Tucker Carlson's Fox News show to discuss her opposition to the Equality Act, federal legislation that would protect sexual orientation and gender identity under civil rights law.[5] In 2017 WoLF formed a coalition with evangelical and anti-abortion group Focus on the Family to oppose trans-inclusive bathroom bills and attempts to interpret Title IX of the Education Act to protect trans rights.[6] WoLF has also been awarded funding by the Alliance Defending Freedom, an anti-abortion organisation that supports recriminalising homosexuality in the US.[7]

WoLF has had support from Republican lawmakers who couch their opposition to trans equality in the language of women's rights. The UK groups Fair Play for Women and A Woman's Place have had similar support, most prominently from the MP for Monmouth David Davies, who has consistently voted for stronger restrictions on abortion, for repealing the Human Rights Act, and against gay marriage. The echoes of colonial feminism here are strong. Another protector of women (only) when it comes to trans people is Carl Benjamin, who was investigated by police after his comments about raping Jess Phillips. In 2019 Benjamin was interviewed by the UKIP Head of Communications Kris Hicks about an alleged attack on journalist Julie Bindel following a University of Edinburgh event on 'women's sex-based rights'. Benjamin condemned the 'level of vitriol' he claimed was coming out of the trans community. UKIP shared the video with the comment: 'The TERFS will all end up joining UKIP.'[8]

There have also been hands across the Atlantic, with growing connections between UK trans-exclusionary feminists, far-right media and the US religious right. In 2018 *Breitbart* supported the UK group Transgender Trend, after its Crowdfunder to develop a school resource pack on the 'trans agenda' was shut down (the funding page was reinstated days later).[9] Conservative Christian groups have also promoted Transgender Trend's social media feed.[10] Catholic feminist Caroline Farrow is a prominent trans-exclusionary figure, and is also the UK Campaign Director for CitizenGo, a conservative petition site linked with 'dark money' from the US and Russia that supports far-right parties in Europe.[11] In 2019 the Women's Liberation Front hosted a group of UK-based trans-exclusionary feminists for a joint meeting with the Heritage Foundation.[12] The Foundation, a conservative think tank staunchly opposed to 'radical feminism', had found common ground with WoLF in its opposition to the Equality Act. This meeting was a step too far for some: a number of prominent trans-exclusionary feminists distanced themselves from alliances with the right. But ideological continuities remain.

## Reactionary feminism and/as conservatism

Many trans-exclusionary and anti-sex-work feminists would put themselves on the left. And there are
certainly strands in reactionary feminism that come
from the radical feminist notion of 'sex class' and the
Marxist critique of commodification.[13] As I described
in Chapter 2, in the radical feminist tradition, wom-
en's reproductive capacities, and men's need to control these capacities, are the original class system. The
sex industry is also born out of male entitlement to
women's bodies, reducing them to objects that can be
owned, bought or sold. These ideas are not obvious
bedfellows of heteropatriarchal conservatism, though
it is easy to see why they do not acknowledge trans
women as women or sex work as work.

The goals of reactionary feminists and conservatives
are also not the same. While conservatives want to
re-impose binary gender, trans-exclusionary feminism,
which often calls itself 'gender-critical', wants to get
rid of it. One of the biggest complaints of 'gender-
critical' feminists is that trans people *reinforce* the
gender binary by transitioning from one side to the
other instead of being masculine women or feminine
men. Non-binary and genderqueer people are
conveniently forgotten here, as is the fact that many
trans people offer passionate critiques of gender as they
navigate it (as we all do) in order to survive. When it
comes to the sex industry, although conservatives and
reactionary feminists both want to eradicate it, this is

for different reasons. Feminists see the industry as a pillar of patriarchy. Religious and paleoconservatives (the patriarchy) blame feminists and queers, because the sex industry symbolises the decline of procreative sex and the heteropatriarchal nuclear family.

But despite these differences, there are many, many similarities. Just as the reactionary magazine *Spiked* (originally called *Living Marxism*) emerged from a Trotskyite splinter group of the International Socialists, reactionary feminism has grown away from its roots. (*Spiked*, which has funding from the ultra-conservative Koch Foundation, is now one of the main outlets currently platforming trans-exclusionary feminists.)[14] Trans-exclusionary feminists and conservatives are both deeply attached to the binary of 'biological sex', despite mounting scientific evidence that sex is more complex than previously thought.[15] For both these groups, sex cannot be changed or traversed: trans women cannot be 'real' women in any biological sense. Conservatives and trans-exclusionary feminists also share with anti-sex-work feminists the idea that the male body is inherently violent, although for conservatives, this only seems to be a problem in relation to men of colour and trans women, and not, for instance, Brett Kavanaugh or Donald Trump.

And notwithstanding trans-exclusionary feminists' claims to be 'gender-critical', these sex-essentialist discussions tend to arrive at gender essentialism in the end. Because in the absence of any mechanism to check chromosomes, or jurisdiction to search people's underwear when allowing them entry into changing rooms or toilets, gender becomes a proxy for sex. Since the most recent iteration of 'trans bathroom panic' in both the US and the UK, a number of cis women have reported being harassed in women's toilets over whether they had any right to be there – because they did not look feminine enough.[16]

To defend this sex and gender essentialism, both conservatives and reactionary feminists appeal to 'science'. But they are actually deeply anti-intellectual in their dismissal of scientific findings that complicate the sex binary. This is also a world where, again discounting evidence to the contrary, simple causal relationships can be drawn between one thing and another. For instance, while conservatives believe that pornography causes teenage pregnancy, some trans-exclusionary feminists believe (citing the discredited concept of 'autogynephilia') that it causes men to want to transition. Anti-sex-work feminists believe that pornography causes rape. 'Pornography is the theory and rape is the practice' is Robin Morgan's famous quote. Slogans like this – and the much-used 'Women Don't Have Penises' (recently written on cartoon penises in a sticker campaign) – fit the contemporary populist era, with its disdain for 'experts' and 'elites' and calls for 'common sense'.

For conservatives, this populism is a deliberate strategy. According to the Southern Poverty Law Center, at the 2017 Values Voter summit (a yearly US conference for conservative activists and politicians), delegates were advised not to use religious arguments against transgender equality. Arguments based on 'biology and reason', they were told, would be more effective.[17] This populist 'common sense' is the foil to the idea of trans people as proponents of the 'gender ideology' also being pushed by feminists and queers to undermine the heterosexual nuclear family. As I wrote in Chapter 1, opposition to 'gender ideology' is a powerful unifying trope for the international far right. And despite its unsavoury connections, reactionary feminists also use the trope of 'gender ideology' in their attacks on trans people.

In 2019 a New Zealand group called Speak Up For Women distributed a petition signed by almost 40,000 people against the teaching of 'gender ideology' in schools. The press release read:

> Of particular concern to Speak Up For Women is the way Ministry of Education-funded gender identity advocacy groups like Rainbow Youth and InsideOUT conflate 'gender identity' with sex. They promote a narrative that denies humans are a sexually dimorphic species, rejects biological sex, and preferences an ever-growing list of imagined genders.

Reactionary feminists and conservatives are united in their view of where these 'imagined genders' come from. The culprit is Gender Studies – specifically, postmodern and queer gender scholarship, because it deconstructs understandings of the body and refuses to treat binary sex as given. Trans-exclusionary feminists call the famous philosopher and queer theorist Judith

Butler 'the high priestess of genderology' and blame her for erasing the category of biological sex. In 2017 the Brazilian religious right burned Butler in effigy outside a conference she had helped to organise.

Postmodernism is a target shared by the 'alt' right, who skewer it as irrational and relativist even as they articulate their own post-truth politics. It is also reviled by members of the intellectual dark web, including Jordan Peterson, who rose to fame after his passionate opposition to a Canadian bill that proposed outlawing discrimination based on gender identity and expression. The bill curtailed free speech, Peterson argued, by requiring the use of gender-affirming pronouns. Pronouns have become a key battleground of the war on 'gender ideology'. They attract extraordinary outrage from people determined to show that others' gender identities are not just socially constructed, but completely made up.

In 2019 over thirty 'gender-critical' UK academics signed an open letter in the *Sunday Times*, arguing that the Stonewall Diversity Champions scheme threatened academic freedom. One of the problems the letter identified was advice to 'ask the pronouns' of students. 'Many of us', the letter read, 'would deny that pronouns refer to an inner feeling of gender identity, and wish to say so.' (In response, over 6,700 current and former university staff signed a letter reaffirming the rights of trans staff and students.) Refusing to call someone what they ask to be called probably seems incredibly petty (and it is). And actions like this highlight how warped reactionary feminism can become: if 'transgenderism' is seen as an ideological delusion, it becomes courageous to refuse to enable it.

Despite the scraps of socialism in its history, this is bourgeois feminism rooted in disdain for those who think and live differently, whose bodies are not easily assimilated to capitalist production and reproduction. Reactionary feminism, like conservatism, is deeply ideological in its policing of 'appropriate' gender and sex. 'Save Our Eyes' is a campaign against the managed prostitution area in the city of Leeds. In this attempt to keep the 'undesirables' out, 'our' eyes will be saved by moving sex workers back into criminalisation. After the Nordic model of client criminalisation was introduced in Ireland in 2017, Irish sex workers reported a 92 per cent increase in violence against them over the course of two years.[18] And for reactionary feminists, this violence is not incidental, but intentional. In 2014 the head of Sweden's Anti-trafficking Unit, Ann Martin, said that violence against sex workers was a desirable effect of 'end demand' policies, acting as a deterrent from entering the industry and an incentive to leave it.[19]

This ideology echoes the conversion therapies for 'fallen women', queers and trans people favoured by the religious right. And the trans woman especially is always already 'fallen', particularly when she is Black because of the historical (and persistent) association between prostitution and Black womanhood. The phrase 'walking while trans' describes how trans women of colour are profiled as sex workers by law enforcement. It was widely used after Black trans woman and activist Monica Jones was found guilty of 'manifesting prostitution' for accepting a car ride from two undercover police officers in Phoenix in 2014. And trans-exclusionary feminism does similar profiling, in campaigns of moral judgement and outrage in which racism, transphobia and hatred of sex workers intersect.

In 2019 the new UK 'gender-critical' organisation Safe Schools Alliance registered objections to the relationship between the National Society for the Prevention of Cruelty to Children (NSPCC) and Black trans model and activist Munroe Bergdorf. Bergdorf had been campaigning for the NSPCC initiative Childline. An open letter by the Safe Schools Alliance said that Bergdorf presented a 'highly sexualised, porn-influenced image' of what it meant to be a woman, and that this 'sent harmful messages to children'. *Times* journalist Janice Turner claimed that Bergdorf was a 'porn model' in a tweet to the NSPCC, which was retweeted and liked over a thousand times. This was a case of walking (or existing) while trans. And together with the suggestion that sex workers posed a threat to children, it created a cocktail of bigoted outrage. The NSPCC cut its ties with Bergdorf immediately.

## Pouring fuel on the fire

While mainstream feminism invests trauma in the outrage economy, reactionary forms fuel the fires with sensationalism and grandstanding. A recent 'gender-critical' protest in London featured graphic photographs of post-surgery trans bodies; anti-sex-work feminists use explicit images and descriptions of violence against sex workers. This is the equivalent of the anti-abortion movement's bloodied foetuses. Andrea Dworkin was an early – and extreme – proponent of this tactic. As author and journalist Charlotte Shane argues, for Dworkin terror was necessary – but her violent language was indistinguishable from misogyny and betrayed a deep hostility towards sex workers.[20] In Dworkin's 1993 speech 'Prostitution and Male Supremacy', Shane writes,

> [she] assumed the mantle of an imagined 'john' and said that 'the prostituted woman' is *nobody real, I don't have to deal with her ... She is perceived as, treated as—and I want you to remember this, this is real—vaginal slime. She is dirty; a lot of men have been there. A lot of semen, a lot of vaginal lubricant ... Her mouth is a receptacle.'*

Anti-trafficking campaigns tell us that 'every two minutes' a child is being prepared for sexual exploitation like this. They tell us 'this could be your daughter'. Or even 'this could be you'. But these claims are based on shaky data.[21] Definitions of sex work, trafficking and migration vary internationally, so there is very little agreement on what should be counted. In some contexts, all migrant women who sell sex are defined as trafficked. In others, it is women who sell sex full stop, or all undocumented migrants. 'Trafficking' is also a blunt instrument to describe the complex relationships between migrants, people who sell sex (and people who fit both these categories) and the various people who facilitate their travel and work. Nevertheless, the myths persist, and the agitation grows.

In 2018 Edgar Welch of Salisbury, North Carolina, was arrested after firing a gun in a pizzeria that he believed was the centre of a 'child sex slave' ring linked with Hillary Clinton.[22] There are echoes here of nineteenth-century 'white slavery' fears, and the 1980s panic about Satanic ritual abuse of children in daycare centres in the US. The terror of Satanic ritual abuse, stoked by the emerging Christian fundamentalist right, coincided with the AIDS crisis and was underpinned by concerns about protecting the heterosexual nuclear family from a number of threats (including women's employment).[23] The idea of 'stranger danger' at the heart of this panic is also at the heart of contemporary fears about trans women in women's space.

And in trans-exclusionary politics, dystopian fantasies reach their peak. In January 2019, at the joint panel with the Heritage Foundation, Women's Liberation Front board member Kara Dansky claimed that if the US Equality Act was passed:

> Male rapists will go to women's prisons and will likely assault female inmates as has already happened in the UK. Female survivors of rape will be unable to contest male presence in women's shelters. Men will dominate women's sports. Girls who would have taken first place will be denied scholastic opportunity. Women who

use male pronouns to talk about men may be arrested, fined, and banned from social media platforms. Girls will stay home from school when they have their periods to avoid harassment by boys in mixed sex toilets. Girls and women will no longer have the right to ask for female medical staff or intimate care providers, including elderly or disabled women who are at serious risk of sexual abuse.

This is a terrible world indeed. But it is not likely to materialise. In countries with gender self-identification, such as Ireland, Malta, Norway and Portugal, there has not been a rash of sex attacks by trans women, or men posing as trans women, in women's spaces. Trans women have not dominated the Olympics and other international sporting events since the 2003 International Olympic Committee guidelines allowed them to compete as women provided they had had sex-reassignment surgery and had undergone two years of hormone therapy (in 2015 the surgery requirement was removed, but trans women still have to reduce their testosterone to approved levels). Other claims, for instance about 'rapid onset gender dysphoria' (which posits that trans children are victims of social contagion) have been similarly debunked.[24]

Reactionary feminists assimilate these critiques, however, as evidence of a conspiracy. Sex workers and their allies are dismissed as the 'pimp lobby'. Trans people and their allies become the 'trans cabal', or in an incredibly offensive formulation, the 'trans Taliban'. There have been comparisons between sex workers and arms dealers, and trans people and 'big pharma', which betray a fascistic tendency to invest the enemy with immense power. And any challenge to reactionary feminist views is repackaged, via these conspiracy theories, as evidence that they are indeed right. Terms such as 'trans Taliban' echo other reactionary monikers, such as the racist 'woke Stasi' and misogynist 'feminazi', which are common on the far right. They also tap the contemporary appetite for conspiracy that has supported recent rightward shifts. Reactionary feminists may well be the *InfoWars* of the movement.

Also from the far-right playbook: claims of being silenced and oppressed. Reactionary feminists (or men speaking on their behalf) have made this claim in many high-profile media outlets. 'We must not silence debate about transgenderism for fear of offending its activists' – James Kirkup, the *Telegraph*. 'Women's groups claim "silencing" on transgender concerns' – Jamie Doward, the *Guardian*. 'Meghan Murphy and the silencing of women' – Ella Whelan, *Spiked*. 'Transgender activists and the real war on women' – Judith Green, *The Spectator*. 'Silencing women in the name of trans activism' – Julie Bindel, *Quillette*. These loud claims about being silenced, made by people with substantial political and institutional clout, are evidence that exactly the opposite is the case. As Sara Ahmed says: 'Whenever people keep being given a platform to say they have no platform, or whenever people speak endlessly about being silenced, you not only have a performative contradiction; you are witnessing a mechanism of power.'[25]

Claiming to be silenced amplifies and circulates reactionary forms of speech by generating outrage. And this manoeuvre works not because reactionary feminists are speaking truth to power and being *accused* of transphobia, but because they are speaking *for* power by expressing transphobia. This is how reactionary feminists, like far-right figures such as Jordan Peterson and Milo Yiannopoulos, have built platforms from claiming they have none.

## Reactionary feminism as capitalist-colonial mentality

Trans-exclusionary and anti-sex-work feminists represent peak political whiteness. They magnify mainstream feminist narcissism, not only centring themselves but also acting as gatekeepers who withhold the designation 'woman' from others. This especially applies to trans women, defined as 'biological men' while trans-exclusionary feminists proclaim themselves 'adult human females' (which leads to policing of other categories such as 'lesbian', reserved for 'adult human females' attracted to each other). And the juxtaposition of sex workers' rights and 'women's safety' implicitly withholds womanhood from sex workers as well. This is a reassertion of the normative economically productive body and reproductive sex. In this bourgeois mentality, neither the 'unnatural' or the 'unrespectable' woman can ever be a real woman.

Instead, these women become the enemy. In reactionary feminism, the alertness to threat that characterises political whiteness becomes a mentality of 'us and them'. They are the trans Taliban; they are the pimp lobby; and they have all the power. Sex workers are described as 'handmaidens of the patriarchy' or even 'orifices for sale'. Trans women are defined as rapists and child abusers who, in Janice Raymond's words, should be 'morally mandated' out of existence.[26] The reactionary feminist will to power is then realised in necropolitics that harms these more marginalised women, under the guise of fighting powerful, conspiratorial lobbies and asserting rightful ownership of womanhood and feminism.

Here, the authoritarian overtones of political whiteness reach a crescendo. Sex workers are deliberately criminalised; trans women are denied access to space and resources, especially in response to the right-wing fable that there is no longer enough to go around. And in its hoarding of resources and shutting of doors, in its defence against the necropolis, reactionary feminism is complicit with the border walls of the right. It also echoes the far right in its weaponisation of 'women's safety' – reactionary feminists are the ultimate wounded white victims. They are endangered as a 'sex class' (by people who are simply trying to survive). They are content to be defended, like property, by men who reserve their own right to perpetrate abuse.

As I highlighted in Chapter 2, the idea of women as a universal 'sex class' is fundamentally white. It has long been critiqued by feminists of colour, because it marginalises race, class and other issues and so can only represent and benefit the most privileged. In 2013 790 individuals and 60 organisations from 41 countries signed a 'Statement of Trans-Inclusive Feminism and Womanism'. Among other things, the statement said: 'By positing "woman" as a coherent, stable identity whose boundaries they are authorized to police, transphobic feminists reject the insights of intersectional analysis, subordinating all other identities to womanhood and all other oppressions to patriarchy.'[27]

Many reactionary feminists have attacked the principle of intersectionality. There have been overt attacks in the feminist 'intersectionality wars' in academic spaces and on social media. There have also been proxy ones: reactionary feminists have supported denunciations of 'identity politics' and Gender Studies by the intellectual dark web and the far right. Writer and critic Flavia Dzodan has argued that such 'Victorian feminist' attacks on intersectionality reflect the anxieties of bourgeois white women faced with ideas and politics generated by former subjects of Empire.[28] In the current economic crisis, they may also reflect the anxieties of class-privileged women faced with Others demanding their share.

Dzodan views trans-exclusionary feminism as a settler-colonial mentality, an attempt to solidify sex and gender categories that sees womanhood as immutable. Its essentialist mindset reflects how 'the coloniser could name us, assign us a place and a role in the hierarchies'. The 'identity politics' it decries pushes back against this order.[29] The claim to ownership of feminism can also be seen as a colonial project. In 2018 Irish feminists wrote an open letter to the 'We Need to Talk' campaign, which had organised a meeting opposing Gender Recognition Act reform (under the guise of talking about abortion) in Dublin. Among other things, the writers objected to the campaign's assertion of feminist authority in their country. 'We have had enough of colonialism in Ireland', the letter read, 'without needing more of it from you.'

Today's reactionary feminists are descendants of nineteenth-century 'vice-fighters', Christian moralists and anti-miscegenationists, the bourgeois women enlisted by Fordism to 'improve' the working class, and those who ran the reformatories for 'wayward' Black girls and who abused them 'for their own good'.[30] And the lineage is not just ideological. The Magdalene Laundries in Ireland, built in the eighteenth century to house 'fallen women', have more recently become Ruhama, an outreach organisation for women in prostitution. Anti-trafficking campaigns were prefigured by the 'white slavery' panics associated with nineteenth-century temperance, underpinned by bourgeois concerns about 'working class drunkenness' and immigration. The fear of 'white slavery' was the fear that bourgeois white women would be exploited by Black and/or 'foreign' men, in saloons linked with prostitution (which was identified with Black women) and working-class and Black political organising.[31] More recently, this 'white innocence' has been set against the (racialised) figures of the trafficker and the pimp.

Contemporary anti-trafficking imagery often features white girls held captive by Black or brown men. As Juno Mac and Molly Smith write, 'he is a dark hand over her mouth or a looming, shadowy figure behind her'. The term 'modern slavery' has replaced 'white slavery', but this rhetoric remains suffused with race: many trafficking initiatives have 'innocence' in their titles, coding their victimised subjects as white.[32] A number of people of colour accompanying white children through US airports have recently been profiled as traffickers. And while they rescue wounded white girls and women, anti-trafficking and modern slavery initiatives legitimise and strengthen border regimes, subjecting undocumented people to surveillance and punitive state action. Mac and Smith are right when they say that anti-trafficking is border policing.

White feminism has a long history of policing the border. Privileged suffrage campaigners positioned votes for women as important to prevent the system being 'overrun' by newly enfranchised African American or working-class white men. Carrie Chapman Catt, the founder of the American League of Women Voters, said: 'white supremacy will be strengthened, not weakened, by women's suffrage'.[33] And as Sophie Lewis points out, many of these feminists also supported eugenic programmes in which privileged white women were encouraged to reproduce while women of other classes and racialised groupings were not (these continue in contemporary campaigns targeting 'overpopulation' in developing countries, protecting bourgeois economic interests from the 'fecundity' of the Other).[34] Marie Stopes was a committed eugenicist, and the name of her organisation was the Society for Constructive Birth Control and Racial Progress (many eugenicists also supported the sterilisation of sex workers, along with disabled people and other groups).[35] The women's section of the British Union of Fascists counted former suffragettes among its members.[36]

Contemporary trans-exclusionary feminism is similarly animated by the fear of being 'overrun'. And this fear is almost always sexualised: reactionary feminists have much in common with conservatives who claim that increased immigration will result in increased rape. Dystopian fantasies of the female and lesbian 'erasure' that will result from trans women being recognised as women sit alongside the Islamophobic conspiracy theory of the 'great replacement' and the antisemitic spectre of 'white genocide' (there is also, incidentally, a theory that 'transactivism' is being funded by George Soros).[37] Traversing borders is a threat – and in the colonial mindset, the borders of class and nationality are at one with the borders of gender. Binary gender is a colonial and capitalist project, what feminist theorist Gloria Anzaldúa called the 'absolute despot duality that says we are able to be only one or the other'.[38]

Western borders are currently being reasserted in the context of economic crisis, to protect the global 'haves' from the 'have-nots'. And reactionary feminism is complicit with this capitalist and neo-colonial project. It foregrounds narratives of scarcity; it claims resources and support for the 'good' women rather than the 'bad'. Sex workers are criminalised and endangered by policies that purport to protect other women from sexual objectification and abuse. Trans women are denied access to the spaces they need for validation and help, or prevented from simply getting on with their lives (for instance, by going to the bathroom). And in the midst of a crisis of social reproduction, the effect is to keep more marginalised women from their own life-making. This is ultimately an eliminationist project.

Trans-exclusionary feminism in particular is one of a number of colonial and arguably eugenicist ideologies currently being resurrected, legitimated and mainstreamed under the banner of 'free speech', 'inquiry' and 'debate'. The crusade against 'gender ideology' is also a crusade to resurrect 'race science', and trans-exclusionary feminists have shared platforms (notably the pseudo-intellectual *Quillette*) with a number of proponents of the latter. For instance right-wing journalist Toby Young, associate editor of *Quillette* and an advocate of 'progressive eugenics',[39] and Noah Carl, the researcher sacked from Cambridge University in 2019. The investigation of Carl's work found that it 'demonstrated poor scholarship, promoted extreme right-wing views and incited racial and religious hatred'.

The crusade against transgender equality also reflects the colonial 'divide and conquer' tactics of the right. In 2017 the US Family Research Council held its annual Values Voter Summit in Washington DC (at which Donald Trump was the first sitting president to speak). At the event, Meg Kilgannon of Concerned Parents and Educators of Fairfax County proposed a strategy to separate the T from the LGB. 'Trans and gender identity are a tough sell', she said, 'so focus on gender identity to divide and conquer.'[40] In June 2015 the Family Research Council had issued a policy paper called 'Understanding and Responding to the Transgender Movement' that quoted extensively from Raymond's *The Transsexual Empire*.

Divide and conquer means that these 'friends' of reactionary feminists will become enemies in the end. And attacks on trans people have already paved the way for attacks on LGBT equality more broadly. Current trans-exclusionary rhetoric echoes that which circulated about Section 28, a clause of the 1988 UK Local Government Act which outlawed the 'promotion of homosexuality' in schools. The Thatcher administration and its supporters justified Section 28 using the language of social contagion and 'grooming', with gay men especially demonised as a threat. And in 2019 a national debate on whether children should have 'LGBT education' began again, following protests by Birmingham parents against an inclusive curriculum initiative. Like supporters of Section 28 over thirty years before, protestors waved banners saying: 'Adam and Eve, not Adam and Steve.'[41] Also in 2019 the US Justice Department filed an amicus brief pertaining to a Supreme Court case, arguing that the term 'sex' in

Title VII of the Civil Rights Act did not protect lesbian, gay and bisexual workers from discrimination. This was hot on the heels of a similar brief arguing that the term 'sex' did not cover gender identity, pertaining to a different case (in this latter case a number of briefs making similar arguments cited blogs and tweets by trans-exclusionary feminists, and a brief was also submitted by the Women's Liberation Front).

There have been many disavowals of trans-exclusionary and anti-sex-work feminism by white feminists (including me) who consider ourselves allies of the trans and sex-working communities. 'This is not our feminism!', we cry. But this is not wholly true. Mainstream white feminism, which uses the corporate media and state/institutional discipline to redress individual injuries, cannot tackle the intersections of heteropatriarchy, racial capitalism and colonialism that produce sexual violence. At the thicker end of this wedge, reactionary feminism is complicit with the far-right politics also produced by this intersectionality of systems. The necropolitics of reactionary feminism is where the political whiteness of the mainstream ends up.

# Conclusion

Reactionary trans-exclusionary and anti-sex-work feminism amplifies the narcissistic 'Me, Not You' of the mainstream. Marginalised people are not only collateral, but are threats impeding the white feminist will to power. This is a colonial and capitalist mentality – engrossed in scarcity narratives, and competitive and ungenerous as a result – which has been empowered in the current economic crisis. Of course, feminists of colour already know this. They will probably have little to learn from the arguments I have presented here. So my conclusion directly addresses the white feminists who may be reading this book. Our task, I think, is not to disavow reactionary perspectives, but to examine how our feminism has produced and enabled them and (most importantly) work towards doing our feminism differently. Especially because restricting ourselves to 'calling out' reactionary feminists can allow us to ignore or erase the impact of political whiteness in the mainstream. Mainstream feminism tends to reinforce the status quo – and this status quo is violent in itself.

## Conclusion

Like political theorist Zillah Eisenstein, I also wonder about the distinction between being an ally and a comrade. Standing with more marginalised women is crucial. But for Eisenstein, allyship means supporting a struggle but not being in or of it, while comradeship implies we are all in this together.[1] Eisenstein's definition of allyship reminds me of the performative outrage of whiteness. To become comrades, by her definition, we would need to spend less time in outrage and more time loosening the knots of political whiteness in ourselves and our politics. We would need to let our ideas and actions be led by more marginalised people. We would need to work against how racial capitalism divides and stratifies us for profit.

Sexual violence is a pivot for the intersecting systems of heteropatriarchy, racial capitalism and colonialism. And politically white feminism, whether mainstream or reactionary, fails to interrogate two of the three. It is complicit with the racial capitalism, and its colonial and neo-colonial expansion, which frames violent and sexually violent abuses of power. Instead of interrogating intersecting systems, politically white feminism roots violence either in aberrant or *all* male bodies. The mainstream focus on 'bad men', and the reactionary focus on male biology, do not account for how capitalist economic predation and misogynist sexual predation go hand in hand. They do not account for how this interplay is racialised, domestically and geopolitically. There is little space here for the rape rampant in Export Processing Zones, the agricultural fields of abused migrant workers, and the 'man camps' of extractive industries. There is little space here for femicide in Latin America, the 'witch-hunts' of dispossessed women in sub-Saharan Africa, and the abuses occurring throughout the care chains that link paid and unpaid female workers across the globe.

To resist an intersectionality of systems, we need what Angela Davis calls an intersectionality of struggles. As Audre Lorde said: 'there is no such thing as a single-issue struggle because we do not live single-issue lives'.[2] What would happen if the white women at the forefront of #MeToo listened to and learned from the Black women, both trans and cis, at the forefront of prison abolition? Or if activists against sexual harassment in universities and other institutions joined forces with sex workers' unions and organisations supporting migrant labourers? What would a campaign against trafficking look like, if it was also a campaign against borders? What would a campaign against sexual exploitation look like, if it was also a campaign against the exploitation of nature? How might we put the fight against sexual violence alongside battles for the essentials of social reproduction, such as water and cleaner air?

This connected politics already exists, of course – and it is from this that we must take our lead. From the Combahee River Collective Statement, the Critical Resistance Statement of Incite! and the work of other radical networks of women and non-binary people of colour. From the Women's Strike, Feminists Rise

Conclusion

Up Against Fascism, and other feminist movements grounded in anti-capitalist, anti-fascist *and anti-racist* struggle. From survivor-centred transformative justice and community accountability processes, in which perpetrators are encouraged to take responsibility for the harm they have caused and move towards new ways of being and relating. Politics such as this can produce what Akwugo Emejulu and Leah Bassel call solidarities of care, focused on the most marginalised because this will ultimately benefit us all.[3] Politics such as this can create hope, in contrast to the fear that underpins political whiteness. This is what Angela Davis calls 'abolition feminism': feminism that opposes, rather than legitimates, oppressive state systems.[4]

I started this book by arguing that we are seeing a huge growth of the globally networked movement of survivors, alongside a rightward political shift linked to economic crisis. This shift involves the expansion of carceral states and more open oppression of marginalised groups, as economies contract and growing populations join the ranks of the hyper-exploited or are placed outside capitalism entirely. And 'women's safety' is being weaponised as part of these processes, to justify attacks on the necropolis. This gives urgency to demands for a transformation in how we address harm. Demands made by organisers such as Mariame Kaba, who has long worked, with other feminists of colour, in the spaces between prison abolition, decarceration and eradicating sexual violence. For these feminists, abolishing the prison-industrial complex

163

means creating alternative forms of accountability and governance that are not based on domination, hierarchy and control.

This is a profound challenge to political whiteness, which is perhaps why most mainstream sexual violence activists have chosen not even to hear it. And as Kaba acknowledges, we are looking at a lot of work: abolishing prisons requires a complete restructuring of society. So does ending sexual violence. But that does not mean our politics cannot imagine, model and *work towards* the society we want. This is what Kaba, with Kelly Hayes, calls a 'jailbreak of the imagination'.[5] And white feminists urgently need to break free. Naming, shaming and punishing repeat the same patriarchal, capitalist and colonial dynamics that produce violence and abuse – they are what Audre Lorde would call the 'master's tools'.[6] And we live in a world where the master is violently reasserting control. We cannot continue to 'wage war' driven by outrage and desire for power; we must not dwell on our own border anxieties while the Western 'we' is violently reconstituted in a futile drive to resurrect Empire. In other words, we need to dismantle power, not merely demand a shift in who wields it.

What might a world without sexual violence look like? That question is worth a book in itself, but let's try a brief thought experiment. Racial capitalism would be over; economic production would support social repro-duction or life-making, not the generation of profit. This could mean an end to binary gender, which is inextricably bound up with racial capitalism and its separation of productive and reproductive spheres. In a world without capitalism, in a world without binary gender, we would rethink relationality and care. There would be diverse forms of intimacy, and what Sophie Lewis calls 'full surrogacy' – a complete collectivisation of biological and social reproduction.[7] We would be concerned with sustaining human and planetary life, not with producing and reproducing workers to maintain dysfunctional economies. If the state continued to exist, its function would be to (re)distribute resources and provide support, not to punish or to wage war. There would not be private property, although lands would have been returned and reparations (of various kinds) made to groups that had been dispossessed and exploited. There would be no national borders. There would be no prisons. There would be accountability, but not vengeance. Social relations would be based on the values of collectivity and care, for each other, for other species and for the planet. The needs that were greatest would be met first. And because of all this, there would not be powerful groups dominating more marginalised ones through violence.

We are not going to live in such a world in my lifetime or yours. But this does not mean we cannot use it to guide our politics *now*. This can be done in eminently practical ways, through advocating for or supporting what prison abolitionists call 'non-reformist reforms'. These are measures that move us towards the society we want. In relation to sexual violence,

these might be transformative justice projects, comprehensive education (not training) programmes on
sex, relationships and violence interruption, initiatives to address dysfunctional institutional or organisational cultures, and freely available survivor-centred
support. We might also advocate for other things: a
universal (and unconditional) living income, affordable
and widespread social housing, an end to private education, free universal childcare and free healthcare for
all (including abortion on demand). One of the main
messages of this book is that white feminists need a
broader view. Politics to end sexual violence needs to
undo the structures that sustain it.

Abolition politics also means refusing to support
reforms that move us further away from our ultimate
goals. This can be a wrench. Scholar and prison abolitionist Ruth Wilson Gilmore gives the example of
opposition from activists within the prison system
to so-called 'gender-responsive' units that would
allow mothers to be locked up with their children –
opposition on the grounds that these would expand,
not shrink, the state's capacity for incarceration.[8] In
the area of sexual violence, abolition politics might
mean opposing new criminal offences created for
'women's protection', for instance 'upskirting' (taking
a photograph up someone's skirt without their permis-
sion), which in 2019 was made a crime punishable
by up to two years in prison in England and Wales
(to loud applause from mainstream feminists). Or the
SHIELD Act currently being proposed in the US (and

backed by Kamala Harris), which would make distributing 'revenge porn' a federal crime. Abolition politics might also mean opposing institutional reforms, for instance policies that make it easier to dismiss harassers, but that chip away at everyone's employment rights. Or state-led metrics that force universities to tackle sexual harassment (and punish those that do not), but contribute to the toxic, competitive, evaluative cultures that help produce it in the first place. In future, abolition politics might require us to refuse increased funding for women's services if this requires trans-exclusionary admissions policies. Or to oppose equality legislation which relies on essentialist definitions of sex and gender.

This type of politics would not tolerate the myopia of political whiteness. It would be hard work, requiring us to ask tough questions about the direction of our demands, about who our friends and allies are, and whether they might not be our friends and allies at all. It would require us to reflect on whether our 'wins' might be others' losses. White feminism is not abolition feminism. But I do not want to dismiss the dynamism and efforts of fellow white women committed to ending sexual violence. What I really want is for us to channel our energies into working against political whiteness in ourselves and in our politics, and into building rather than tearing down.

As Ruth Wilson Gilmore says, abolition is not about tearing down – it is 'figuring out how to work with people to make something rather than figuring out how to erase something'.[9] Instead of using the white feminist wrecking ball, we should *build towards* a world without sexual violence. This is not about forgiveness, empathy or being 'nice' – it is about the fact that we cannot end violence by *doing violence*. Even – no, especially – if that violence manifests as tears.

Inspired by Sara Ahmed's 'killjoy survival kit' from her book *Living a Feminist Life*, I end with a toolkit for fellow white feminists. It consists of six questions we can ask ourselves and our white peers, whether we are doing direct action, legal advocacy, policy development, peer support or other 'everyday' forms of politics and disruption. These questions, if asked consistently and sincerely, might move us towards an abolition feminist mindset and inform different forms of political action. I hope they might help us to achieve what Ahmed calls turning both towards and away from whiteness (and ourselves) – addressing our role in and responsibility for racism while focusing our political action on more marginalised people.[10] The questions are not exhaustive, and we should not punish ourselves if we fail to ask them every time (not least because white guilt is just another way of taking up space and avoiding accountability through seeking reassurance). But it is imperative to try.

1. What do I know?
*Am I educated enough to be making an intervention on this issue? If not, how can I educate myself? And if*

not, are there already people in the field I can support constructively, with my time and/or money? (with thanks to Mariame Kaba, via Twitter, for the preceding questions).

## 2. Who am I speaking for?

Am I primarily speaking for myself? How much space do I occupy with my own experiences, needs and views? Can I listen to others, even if they challenge me? Am I using my own experiences to silence critics? If I speak for others, am I qualified? Am I using others' experiences to win arguments or get my own way? Can I step back and let more marginalised people speak for themselves? Can I step back and let more marginalised people lead?

## 3. Who benefits?

Am I making political demands that will primarily benefit people like me? Are my needs and demands shared by those in more marginalised positions? If not, might meeting my needs and demands bring harm or suffering to those people? Can I broaden my political frame to develop demands and actions that benefit us all? Can I let my politics be led by the needs and demands of more marginalised people?

## 4. What are my motivations?

Do I want accountability or revenge? Do I want attention? Do I want power? How do my desires drive my politics? How can I acknowledge and work through less helpful feelings, to ensure they are not in the driving seat? While acknowledging my own anger, am I also receptive to that of others, even when it is directed at me? How can I make productive, rather than vindictive, use of my anger? Am I seeking the quick ego-boost of performative outrage? How can I turn outrage into action?

5. Who am I with?
*Am I an ally or a comrade to more marginalised people? Who are MY allies, and why? Where can strategic alliances be made, and where is this impossible? If I am prepared to ally myself strategically with people I would normally reject outright, why am I prepared to do this? Who might this harm?*

6. Where are we going?
*Does my/our activism make small steps towards a world without sexual violence? Or does it take steps further away? Does it diminish, or increase, the violent capacities of the state and/or institution? If my demands do not move things forward, why am I going ahead? Can I be brave enough to resist or refuse reforms which do not move things forward, even if this causes me pain? Can I be brave enough to take small steps towards a society that would be better for us all?*

In ending the book this way, I am taking a risk: these questions could appear 'navel-gazing' at first glance, an enactment of political whiteness or what Lauren Michele Jackson calls 'white-on-white pontificating'.[11] But my intention is for them to inform and frame political *action* in which privileged white feminists take their lead from more marginalised people. I do not want to centre white feminists and our problems; I want to expand our capacity to deal with them without expecting others in our political communities (and women of colour especially) to do the work for us. I give my final question to Audre Lorde, who did so much of this work during her lifetime; this was posed in her 1981 keynote speech at the National Women's Studies Association conference.

# Conclusion

> What woman here is so enamoured of her own
> oppression that she cannot see her heelprint on another
> woman's face?[12]

Almost forty years later, this question is still crucially
relevant to the mainstream feminist fight against
sexual violence. It is high time we answered it.

# Notes

1 Black feminism has been essential to the development of this book. But I do not intend to fetishise Black feminists as the 'saviours' of feminism, as they are often now imagined to be – Jennifer Nash's book *Black Feminism Reimagined: After Intersectionality* (Durham, NC: Duke University Press) is an excellent discussion of this dynamic.

2 Throughout the book, I use the terms Black, brown and women of colour at different times. This is because at times it makes sense to refer to all women of colour as a group (for instance, when racism treats them that way), and at times it is necessary to describe specific experiences and forms of politics. The category of Black (which I use to refer to people of African and African-Caribbean descent) is particularly important to distinguish, due to the specific history of enslavement and the existence of anti-Black racism in other communities of colour. I follow the convention of capitalising the 'B' in Black to denote that Black people are a people: Black is a cultural and political identity (I also capitalise the 'I' in Indigenous for similar reasons). 'Political Blackness' has been used to describe the unification of all non-white people under the term 'Black'; this is largely a British concept (and not uncontested), and has influenced some Black British feminism.

3 Sara Ahmed, 'Declarations of whiteness: the non-performativity of anti-racism', *Borderlands* 3:2 (2004),

http://www.borderlands.net.au/vol3no2_2004/ahmed_dec larations.htm (accessed 1 November 2019).

4 I have referenced a number of key academic sources for those who wish to follow up with further reading. I have also referenced some of my background evidence, particularly where I make specific claims or refer to incidents that have not been widely reported or are not common knowledge.

5 Sara Ahmed, *Willful Subjects* (Durham, NC: Duke University Press, 2014), p. 6.

6 Sara Ahmed, *Living a Feminist Life* (Durham, NC: Duke University Press, 2017), p. 16.

7 Sarah Banet-Weiser, *Empowered: Popular Feminism and Popular Misogyny* (Durham, NC: Duke University Press, 2018).

8 Catherine Rottenberg, *The Rise of Neoliberal Feminism* (Oxford: Oxford University Press, 2018); bell hooks, 'Dig deep: beyond lean in', *Feminist Wire*, 28 October 2013; Cinzia Arruzza, Tithi Bhattacharya and Nancy Fraser, *Feminism for the 99%: A Manifesto* (London: Verso, 2019).

9 Kimberlé Crenshaw, 'Mapping the margins: intersectionality, identity politics, and violence against women of color', *Stanford Law Review* 43:6 (1991), 1241–1299.

10 Maria Mies, *Patriarchy and Accumulation on a World Scale: Women in the International Division of Labour* (London: Zed Books, 1986), p. 110.

11 Gargi Bhattacharyya, *Rethinking Racial Capitalism: Questions of Reproduction and Survival* (London: Rowman and Littlefield International, 2018). The term 'racial capitalism' was coined by Cedric Robinson in his important text *Black Marxism: The Making of the Black Radical Tradition* (London: Zed Books, 1983).

12 Saidiya V. Hartman, *Scenes of Subjection: Terror, Slavery and Self-making in Nineteenth-century America* (Oxford: Oxford University Press, 1997).

13 Silvia Federici, *Caliban and the Witch: Women, the Body, and Primitive Accumulation* (New York: Autonomedia, 2004).

14 Amanda Kaladelfos, 'The politics of punishment: rape and

the death penalty in colonial Australia, 1841–1901', *History Australia* 9:1 (2012), 155–175 (pp. 159, 168).

15 Tim Madigan, *The Burning: Massacre, Destruction and the Tulsa Race Riot of 1921* (New York: Thomas Dunne Books, 2001).

### CHAPTER 1

1 An earlier version of this chapter appeared as Alison Phipps, 'The fight against sexual violence', *Soundings* 71 (2019), 62–74.

2 Anita Hill, *Speaking Truth to Power* (New York: Anchor Books, 1997), p. 2.

3 Benjamin L. Hooks, NAACP and Julian Bond, 'The NAACP position on Clarence Thomas', *The Black Scholar* 22:1/2 (1991), 144–150 (p. 144).

4 Barbara Palmer, 'Ten years later, Anita Hill revisits the Clarence Thomas controversy', *Stanford Report*, 3 April 2002, https://news.stanford.edu/news/2002/april3/anitahill-43.html (accessed 1 November 2019).

5 Moya Bailey and Trudy, 'On misogynoir: citation, erasure and plagiarism', *Feminist Media Studies* 18:4 (2018), 762–768.

6 See Saidiya Hartman's book *Wayward Lives, Beautiful Experiments: Intimate Histories of Social Upheaval* (New York: W. W. Norton, 2019) for a brilliant and compelling history of how these constructions shaped the lives of young Black women in Northern US cities in the late nineteenth and early twentieth centuries.

7 Clifford Krauss, 'Anita Hill to Christine Blasey Ford: "Don't do anything that will dehumanize you"', *New York Times*, 28 September 2018, https://www.nytimes.com/2018/09/28/us/anita-hill-metoo-houston.html (accessed 1 November 2019).

8 For more in-depth discussion of neoliberalism, see the following texts: Lisa Duggan, *The Twilight of Equality: Neoliberalism, Cultural Politics, and the Attack on Democracy* (Boston: Beacon Press, 2003); David Harvey, *A Brief History of Neoliberalism* (Oxford: Oxford University

Press, 2005); Colin Crouch, *The Strange Non-death of Neoliberalism* (Hoboken, NJ: John Wiley and Sons, 2011); Wendy Brown, *Undoing the Demos: Neoliberalism's Stealth Revolution* (New York: Zone Books, 2015).

9  Silvia Federici, *Witches, Witch-Hunting and Women* (Oakland, CA: PM Press, 2018), pp. 47–49. See also Tithi Bhattacharya's edited collection *Social Reproduction Theory: Remapping Class, Recentering Oppression* (London: Pluto Press, 2017).

10  Nancy Fraser, 'Crisis of care? On the social-reproductive contradictions of contemporary capitalism', in Tithi Bhattacharya (ed.), *Social Reproduction Theory: Remapping Class, Recentering Oppression* (London: Pluto Press, 2019), pp. 40–60.

11  Federici, *Witches, Witch-Hunting and Women*, p. 50.

12  Bhattacharyya, *Rethinking Racial Capitalism*, p. 141.

13  Fraser, 'Crisis of care?', p. 45.

14  Erin Sanders McDonagh, Lucy Neville and Sevasti-Melissa Nolas, 'From pillar to post: understanding the victimisation of women and children who experience domestic violence in an age of austerity', *Feminist Review* 112:1 (2016), 60–76. See also Maya Oppenheim, 'Domestic violence victims face toughest Christmas yet as cuts leave therapeutic support at all-time low', *Independent*, 22 December 2018, https://www.independent.co.uk/news/uk/home-news/dom estic-violence-victims-christmas-therapeutic-support-vic tims-cuts-refuges-womens-aid-a8673071.html (accessed 1 November 2019).

15  Claire Provost, 'Revealed: Trump-linked US Christian "fundamentalists" pour millions of "dark money" into Europe, boosting the far right', *Open Democracy*, 27 March 2019, https://www.opendemocracy.net/en/5050/revealed-trump-linked-us-christian-fundamentalists-pour-millions-of-dark-money-into-europe-boosting-the-far-right/ (accessed 1 November 2019).

16  Maria Lugones, 'The coloniality of gender', *Worlds and Knowledges Otherwise* 2 (2008), 1–17.

17  Survival International, 'What Brazil's president, Jair Bolsonaro, has said about Brazil's Indigenous Peoples',

https://www.survivalinternational.org/articles/3540-Bolson aro (accessed 15 October 2019).

18  Eliza Apperly, 'Why Europe's far right is targeting Gender Studies', *The Atlantic*, 15 June 2019, https://www.theat lantic.com/international/archive/2019/06/europe-far-right-target-gender-studies/591208/ (accessed 1 November 2019).

19  Matthew Weaver, 'Jordan Peterson launches anti-censorship site Thinkspot', *Guardian*, 13 June 2019, https://www.theguardian.com/technology/2019/jun/13/jordan-peterson-launches-anti-censorship-site-thinkspot (accessed 1 November 2019).

20  James A. Lindsay, Peter Boghossian and Helen Pluckrose, 'Academic grievance studies and the corruption of scholarship', *Areo*, 2 October 2018, https://areomagazine.com/2018/10/02/academic-grievance-studies-and-the-corruption-of-scholarship/ (accessed 1 November 2019).

21  Everytown for Gun Safety, *Mass Shootings in the United States: 2009–2017*, https://everytownresearch.org/reports/mass-shootings-analysis/ (accessed 15 October 2019).

22  For more background, see Stephen J. Baele, 'From "incel" to "saint": analyzing the violent worldview behind the 2018 Toronto attack', *Terrorism and Political Violence* DOI: 10.1080/09546553.2019.1638256 (accessed 15 October 2019).

23  Peter Walker, 'Ukip MEP candidate blamed feminists for rise in misogyny', *Guardian*, 22 April 2019, https://www.theguardian.com/politics/2019/apr/22/ukip-mep-candidate-carl-benjamin-blamed-feminists-for-rise-in-male-violence (accessed 1 November 2019).

24  Asa Bennet and Ned Simons, 'Ukip's new EU ally joked about wife beating and defended Hitler', *Huffington Post*, 20 October 2014, https://www.huffingtonpost.co.uk/2014/10/20/ukip-robert-jaroslaw-iwaszkiewicz-_n_6015116.html (accessed 1 November 2019).

25  Jim Waterson, 'Boris Johnson: police called to loud altercation at potential PM's home', *Guardian*, 21 June 2019, https://www.theguardian.com/politics/2019/jun/21/police-called-to-loud-altercation-at-boris-johnsons-home (accessed 1 November 2019).

# Notes

26 Edwin Hayward, 'Boris Johnson: 14 "lowlights" from 23 years of sexism and chauvinism', *Descrier News*, 23 July 2019, https://descrier.co.uk/politics/boris-johnson-14-low lights-from-23-years-of-sexism-and-chauvinism/ (accessed 1 November 2019).

27 Meaghan Beatley, 'The shocking rape trial that galvanised Spain's feminists – and the far right', *Guardian*, 23 April 2019, https://www.theguardian.com/world/2019/apr/23/wolf-pack-case-spain-feminism-far-right-vox (accessed 1 November 2019).

28 Sian Harrison, 'Protests outside court after Tommy Robinson convicted over video footage', *Belfast Telegraph*, 6 July 2019, https://www.belfasttelegraph.co.uk/news/northern-ireland/protests-outside-court-after-tommy-robin son-convicted-over-video-footage-38286235.html (accessed 1 November 2019).

29 J. R. Thorpe, 'This is how many people have posted "Me Too" since October, according to new data', *Bustle*, 1 December 2017, https://www.bustle.com/p/this-is-how-many-people-have-posted-me-too-since-october-according-to-new-data-6753697 (accessed 1 November 2019).

30 Srila Roy, '#MeToo is a crucial moment to revisit the history of Indian feminism', *Economic and Political Weekly* 53:42 (2018), https://www.epw.in/engage/article/metoo-crucial-moment-revisit-history-indian-feminism (accessed 1 November 2019).

31 Andrea Johnson, Kathryn Menefee and Ramya Sekaran, *Progress in Advancing Me Too Workplace Reforms in #20StatesBy2020* (Washington, DC: National Women's Law Center, 2019).

32 Angela Davis, *Freedom is a Constant Struggle: Ferguson, Palestine and the Origins of a Movement* (Chicago: Haymarket Books, 2016), p. 25.

## Chapter 2

1 Monica Anderson and Skye Toor, *How Social Media Users Have Discussed Sexual Harassment Since #MeToo Went Viral* (Washington, DC: Pew Research Center, 2018).

## Notes

2 Lydia Manikonda, Ghazaleh Beigi, Huan Liu and Subbaro Kambhampati, 'Twitter for sparking a movement, Reddit for sharing the moment: #MeToo through the lens of social media', https://arxiv.org/abs/1803.08022 (accessed 15 October 2019).

3 For an excellent discussion of the dynamics of 'speaking out' in feminism, see Tanya Serisier, *Speaking Out: Feminism, Rape and Narrative Politics* (Basingstoke: Palgrave Macmillan, 2018).

4 Harriet Desmoines and Catherine Nicholson, *Sinister Wisdom 6* (Lincoln, NE: Sinister Wisdom, 1978).

5 Tressie McMillan Cottom, 'Black cyberfeminism: ways forward for intersectionality and digital sociology', in Jessie Daniels, Karen Gregory and Tressie McMillan Cottom (eds), *Digital Sociologies* (Bristol: Bristol University Press, 2016), pp. 211–232.

6 Susan Brownmiller, *Against Our Will: Men, Women and Rape* (London: Penguin, 1976 [1975]), p. 397.

7 For discussion of the history of the hashtag, see Jessie Daniels, 'The trouble with white feminism: whiteness, digital feminism and the intersectional internet', in Safiya Umoja Noble and Brendesha M. Tynes (eds), *The Intersectional Internet: Race, Sex, Class and Culture Online* (New York: Peter Lang, 2016), pp. 41–60.

8 Roisin O'Connor, 'Lena Dunham admits she lied to discredit actor Aurora Perrineau's rape accusation', *Independent*, 6 December 2018, https://www.independent.co.uk/arts-entertainment/tv/news/lena-dunham-aurora-perrineau-apology-rape-murray-miller-hollywood-reporter-a8669846.html (accessed 1 November 2019).

9 Phillips had previously defended the Labour shadow Minister for Women and Equalities Sarah Champion, who wrote an article for the *Sun* entitled 'Britain has a problem with British Pakistani men raping and exploiting white girls'. For further discussion, see Nadya Ali, 'Jess Phillips, Lena Dunham and white feminism', *Media Diversified*, https://mediadiversified.org/2018/02/06/jess-phillips-lena-dunham-and-white-feminism/ (accessed 15 October 2019).

10 Aimee Allison, 'Women of color will hold Joe Biden

accountable', *The Nation*, 10 April 2019, https://www.the
nation.com/article/joe-biden-lucy-flores-women-of-color/
(accessed 1 November 2019).

11 For an excellent discussion of the history of white women
and racism, see Vron Ware, *Beyond the Pale: White Women,
Racism and History* (London: Verso, 1992).

12 Radhika Sanghani, 'The uncomfortable truth about racism
and the suffragettes', *Telegraph*, 6 October 2015, https://
www.telegraph.co.uk/women/womens-life/11914757/Rac
ism - and - the - suffragettes - the - uncomfortable - truth . html
(accessed 1 November 2019).

13 In 2011 there was an outcry after a photo was circulated of a
white woman at the New York City Slutwalk, holding a sign
which read 'Woman is the N*gger of the World' (the title of
a 1972 song by John Lennon and Yoko Ono praised for its
'positive image of women' by the US National Organization
for Women). Black women have roundly critiqued the
comparison of patriarchy to slavery. The equation between
gender and race erases Black women's simultaneous
struggles with the two categories, and co-opts painful Black
histories and slurs to advance the rights of white women
(who have been, and are, complicit in racist oppression).

14 Catharine A. MacKinnon, *Toward a Feminist Theory of the
State* (Cambridge, MA: Harvard University Press, 1989),
p. 12.

15 Shulamith Firestone, *The Dialectic of Sex: The Case for
Feminist Revolution* (London: Verso, 2015 [1970]), pp. 19–20.

16 Susan Griffin, *Rape: The Politics of Consciousness* (San
Francisco: Harper and Row, 1979).

17 Liz Kelly, *Surviving Sexual Violence* (Minneapolis, MN:
University of Minnesota Press, 1988).

18 Brownmiller, *Against Our Will*, pp. 14–15.

19 Kate Millett, *Sexual Politics* (Chicago: University of Illinois
Press, 2000 [1970]), p. 25.

20 Andrea Dworkin, *Intercourse* (New York: Basic Books, 2006
[1987]), pp. 155–156.

21 Emi Koyama, *Whose Feminism Is It Anyway? And Other
Essays from the Third Wave* (Portland, OR: Confluere
Publications, 2004), p. 25.

22 Millett, *Sexual Politics*, p. 23.

23 Germaine Greer, *The Female Eunuch* (London: MacGibbon and Kee, 1970).

24 For a full discussion of gender and class dynamics in European colonialism, see Anne McClintock, *Imperial Leather: Race, Gender and Sexuality in the Colonial Contest* (London: Routledge, 1995). I use 'working-class white' rather than 'white working-class' because Western working classes have always had a high proportion of people of colour. I also do not want to play into the idea of a victimised 'white working class' which is central to contemporary right-wing movements.

25 Elizabeth Bernstein, 'Militarized humanitarianism meets carceral feminism: the politics of sex, rights, and freedom in contemporary antitrafficking campaigns', *Signs* 36:1 (2010), 45–71 (p. 54).

26 Valerie Amos and Pratibha Parmar, 'Challenging imperial feminism', *Feminist Review* 17 (1984), 3–19 (p. 14).

27 Janet E. Halley, Prabha Kotiswaran, Rachel Rebouché and Hila Shamir, *Governance Feminism: An Introduction* (Minneapolis, MN: University of Minnesota Press, 2018).

28 Kristin Bumiller, *In an Abusive State: How Neoliberalism Appropriated the Feminist Movement against Sexual Violence* (Durham, NC: Duke University Press, 2008).

29 Leila Ahmed, *Women and Gender in Islam* (New Haven, CT: Yale University Press, 1992), p. 151.

30 Gayatri Spivak, 'Can the subaltern speak? Speculations on widow sacrifice', *Wedge* 7–8 (1985), 120–130.

31 Gargi Bhattacharyya, *Dangerous Brown Men: Exploiting Sex, Violence and Feminism in the 'War on Terror'* (London: Zed Books, 2008), p. 18.

32 Bernstein, 'Militarized humanitarianism meets carceral feminism', p. 53.

33 Lila Abu-Lughod, 'Do Muslim women really need saving? Anthropological reflections on cultural relativism and its others', *American Anthropologist* 104:3 (2002), 783–790 (p. 787).

34 Crenshaw, 'Mapping the margins'.

35 Amii Larkin Barnard, 'The application of Critical Race

feminism to the anti-lynching movement: Black women's fight against race and gender ideology, 1892–1920', *UCLA Women's Law Journal* 3 (1993), 1–38.

36 Angela Y. Davis, *Violence against Women and the Ongoing Challenge to Racism* (New York: Women of Color Press, 1985), pp. 9–10.

37 Hartman, *Wayward Lives.*

38 In the UK, the idea and practice of political Blackness meant that Black feminism often included feminists of South Asian descent and other feminists of colour. The famous text *Black British Feminism*, edited by Heidi Safia Mirza (London: Routledge, 1997), included Sara Ahmed, Gargi Bhattacharyya and Pragna Patel.

39 For a thorough discussion of these issues, see Sarah Deer, *The Beginning and End of Rape: Confronting Sexual Violence in Native America* (Minneapolis, MN: University of Minnesota Press, 2015).

40 June Namias, *White Captives* (Chapel Hill, NC: University of North Carolina Press, 1993), p. 25.

41 Bhattacharyya, *Rethinking Racial Capitalism*, p. x.

42 Jemma Tosh and Maya Gislason, 'Fracking is a feminist issue: an intersectional ecofeminist commentary on natural resource extraction and rape', *Psychology of Women Section Review* 18:1 (2016), 54–59.

43 André B. Rosay, *Violence Against American Indian and Alaska Native Women and Men* (Washington, DC: National Institute of Justice, 2016).

44 #MeToo has also been taken up by minoritised groups in the Global South, for instance by Dalit feminists in India.

### CHAPTER 3

1 An earlier version of this chapter appeared as Alison Phipps, 'Every woman knows a Weinstein: political whiteness and white woundedness in #MeToo and public feminisms around sexual violence', *Feminist Formations* 31:2 (2019), 1–25.

2 Kelly Hayes and Mariame Kaba, 'The sentencing of Larry

# Notes

Nassar was not "transformative justice". Here's why', *The Appeal*, 5 February 2018, https://theappeal.org/the-sentenc ing-of-larry-nassar-was-not-transformative-justice-here-s-why-a2ea323a6645/ (accessed 1 November 2019).

3 Clare Hemmings, *Why Stories Matter: The Political Grammar of Feminist Theory* (Durham, NC: Duke University Press, 2011).

4 Daniel Martinez HoSang, *Racial Propositions: Ballot Initiatives and the Making of Postwar California* (Berkeley, CA: University of California Press, 2010).

5 Banet-Weiser, *Empowered*, p. 3

6 Kehinde Andrews, 'Don't be fooled by Johnson's "diverse" cabinet. Tory racism hasn't changed', *Guardian*, 25 July 2019, https://www.theguardian.com/commentisfree/2019/ jul/25/johnson-diverse-cabinet-tory-racism-ethnic-minor ity-ministers (accessed 1 November 2019).

7 See, for example, Derek Hook, 'Retrieving Biko: a black consciousness critique of whiteness', *African Identities* 9:1 (2011), 19–32. See also Cheryl E. Matias, *Feeling White: Whiteness, Emotionality, and Education* (Leiden: Brill, 2016), pp. 69–81.

8 Sara Ahmed, 'A phenomenology of whiteness', *Feminist Theory* 8:2 (2007), 149–168 (p. 158).

9 Robin DiAngelo, 'White fragility', *International Journal of Critical Pedagogy* 3:3 (2011), 54–70 (p. 59). For other discussions of the dynamics of whiteness, see the following texts: Tressie McMillan Cottom, *Thick and Other Essays* (New York: New Press, 2019), esp. ch. 4, 'Know Your Whites'; Ruth Frankenberg, *White Women, Race Matters: The Social Construction of Whiteness* (Minneapolis, MN: University of Minnesota Press, 1993); Paula Rothenberg (ed.), *White Privilege: Essential Readings on the Other Side of Racism* (New York: Worth, 2002).

10 Gurminder Bhambra, 'Brexit, Trump and "methodological whiteness": on the misrecognition of race and class', *British Journal of Sociology* 68:S1 (2017), S214-S232.

11 Hazel Carby, 'White woman listen! Black feminism and the boundaries of sisterhood', in Centre for Contemporary Cultural Studies, *The Empire Strikes Back: Race and*

*Racism in Seventies Britain* (London: Hutchinson, 1982), pp. 212–235.

12 Catharine MacKinnon, 'What is a white woman anyway?', *Yale Journal of Law & Feminism* 4:1 (1991), 13–22.

13 Tracy McVeigh and Edward Helmore, 'Feminists fall out over "violent, misogynistic" Rihanna video', *Guardian*, 4 July 2015, https://www.theguardian.com/music/2015/jul/04/feminists-fall-out-over-rihanna-video (accessed 1 November 2019).

14 Mia McKenzie, 'This is what Rihanna's BBHMM video says about Black women, white women and feminism', http://www.bgdblog.org/2015/07/this-is-what-rihannas-bbhmm-video-says-about-black-women-white-women-and-feminism/ (accessed 3 July 2015).

15 Audre Lorde, *Sister Outsider: Essays and Speeches* (Berkeley, CA: Crossing Press, 2007 [1984]), p. 126.

16 William C. Anderson and Zoé Samudzi, *As Black as Resistance: Finding the Conditions for Liberation* (Chico, CA: AK Press, 2018), p. 78.

17 Reni Eddo-Lodge, *Why I'm No Longer Talking to White People about Race* (London: Bloomsbury, 2017), p. 170.

18 Mamta Motwani Accapadi, 'When white women cry: how white women's tears oppress women of color', *The College Student Affairs Journal* 26:2 (2007), 208–215; Ruby Hamad, *White Tears, Brown Scars* (Melbourne: Melbourne University Press, 2019), esp. ch. 5.

19 Rowena Mason, 'Theresa May "allowed state-sanctioned abuse of women" at Yarl's Wood', *Guardian*, 3 March 2015, https://www.theguardian.com/uk-news/2015/mar/03/yarls-wood-may-state-sanctioned-abuse-women (accessed 1 November 2019).

20 Jamilah Lemieux, 'Weinstein, white tears and the boundaries of Black women's empathy', *Cassius*, 2 November 2017, https://cassiuslife.com/33564/white-women-dont-look-out-for-black-victims/ (accessed 1 November 2019).

21 Jenny Sharpe, 'The unspeakable limits of rape: colonial violence and counter-insurgency', *Genders* 18 (1991), 25–46.

22 After his murder, Emmett Till became an icon of the Civil Rights movement, largely due to the actions of his mother,

Mamie Till-Mobley, who insisted on an open coffin at his funeral. Till's killers were acquitted by an all-white jury, but admitted their guilt in a magazine interview in 1956 (and were protected from further criminal charges because of double jeopardy).

23 Jessie Daniels, 'The word of a white woman can still get Black people killed', *Huffington Post*, 18 July 2018, https://www.huff post.com/entry/opinion-daniels-emmett-till-case_n_5b4e4a ace4b0b15aba8972d4 (accessed 1 November 2019).

24 Hartman, *Scenes of Subjection*, p. 80.

25 Rebecca Epstein, Jamila J. Blake and Thalia González, *Girlhood Interrupted: The Erasure of Black Girls' Childhood* (Georgetown Law Center on Poverty and Inequality, 2017).

26 Susan Griffin, 'Rape: the all-American crime', *Ramparts*, September 1971, 26–35 (p. 26).

27 Barbara Kingsolver, '#MeToo isn't enough. Now women need to get ugly', *Guardian*, 16 January 2018, https://www.theguardian.com/commentisfree/2018/jan/16/metoo-women-daughters-harassment-powerful-men (accessed 1 November 2019).

28 Melissa Gira Grant, 'The unsexy truth about harassment', in *Where Freedom Starts: Sex, Power, Violence in #MeToo* (London: Verso, 2018), pp. 140–146 (p. 141), https://www.versobooks.com/books/2773-where-freedom-starts-sex-power-violence-metoo (accessed 15 October 2019).

29 Jane Ward, 'Bad Girls: on being the accused', in *Where Freedom Starts*, pp. 127–133 (p. 132).

30 Lugones, 'The coloniality of gender', p. 15.

31 Nicole Westmarland and Sue Alderson, 'The health, mental health, and well-being benefits of rape crisis counselling', *Journal of Interpersonal Violence* 28:17 (2013), 3265–3282.

32 Elizabeth Adetiba and Tarana Burke, 'Tarana Burke says #MeToo should center marginalized communities', in *Where Freedom Starts*, pp. 8–37 (p. 14).

33 Meg Sri, 'Feminist groups are right to rally against the Brock Turner-inspired crime bill', *Feministing*, 15 September 2016, http://feministing.com/2016/09/15/feminist-groups-are-right-to-rally-against-the-brock-turner-inspired-crime-bill/ (accessed 1 November 2019).

# Notes

34 For an excellent discussion of mainstream feminism's approach to the sex industry, see Juno Mac and Molly Smith, *Revolting Prostitutes: The Fight for Sex Workers' Rights* (London: Verso, 2018).

## CHAPTER 4

1 Banet-Weiser, *Empowered*, p. 4.

2 Jodi Dean, 'Communicative capitalism: circulation and the foreclosure of politics', *Cultural Politics* 1:1 (2005), 51–74 (p. 55).

3 Jeffrey M. Berry and Sarah Sobieraj, *The Outrage Industry: Political Opinion Media and the New Incivility* (Oxford: Oxford University Press, 2014), p. 5.

4 Karin Wahl-Jorgensen, Andrew Williams, Richard Sambrook, Janet Harris, Iñaki Garcia-Blanco, Lina Dencik, Stephen Cushion, Cynthia Carter and Stuart Allan, 'The future of journalism', *Digital Journalism* 4:7 (2016), 809–815.

5 Ashley 'Dotty' Charles, 'As a Black, gay woman I have to be selective in my outrage. So should you', *Guardian*, 25 January 2018, https://www.theguardian.com/commentis free/2018/jan/25/black-gay-woman-selective-outrage-hash tag-protest-social-media (accessed 1 November 2019).

6 Ann Cahill, *Rethinking Rape* (Ithaca, NY: Cornell University Press, 2001), p. 111.

7 Dean, 'Communicative capitalism', p. 63.

8 Richard Adams, 'Cambridge gives role to academic accused of racist stereotyping', *Guardian*, 7 December 2018, https://www.theguardian.com/world/2018/dec/07/cambridge-gives-role-to-academic-accused-of-racist-stereotyping (accessed 1 November 2019).

9 Max Larkin, 'After outcry about his role in Flint's water crisis, former Michigan gov. Rick Snyder withdraws from Harvard post', *Edify*, 3 July 2019, https://www.wbur.org/edify/2019/07/03/after-outcry-over-his-role-in-flints-water-crisis-former-michigan-gov-rick-snyder-withdraws-from-harvard-post (accessed 1 November 2019).

10 Paul Hitlin, *We the People: Five Years of Online Petitions* (Washington, DC: Pew Research Center, 2016).

# Notes

11 Katie O'Malley, '5 feminist petitions you can sign in under 5 minutes to commemorate International Women's Day', *Elle*, 8 March 2018, https://www.elle.com/uk/life-and-cul ture/culture/news/a42205/feminist-petitions-international-womens-day/ (accessed 1 November 2019).

12 Mary Maxfield, 'History retweeting itself: imperial feminist appropriations of "Bring Back Our Girls"', *Feminist Media Studies* 16:5 (2016), 886–900.

13 Lauren Berlant,'The subject of true feeling: pain, privacy and politics', in Sara Ahmed, Jane Kilby, Celia Lury, Beverley Skeggs and Maureen McNeil (eds), *Transformations: Thinking through Feminism* (London: Routledge, 2000), pp. 33–47 (p. 35).

14 Jacob Stolworthy, 'James Franco accused of sexual misconduct after accepting Golden Globes award in "Time's Up" pin', *Independent*, 9 January 2018, https://www.inde pendent.co.uk/arts-entertainment/james-franco-golden-glo bes-2018-sexual-harassment-times-up-the-disaster-artist-a8 149191.html (accessed 1 November 2019).

15 Sara Ahmed and Jackie Stacey, 'Testimonial cultures: an introduction', *Cultural Values* 5:1 (2001), 1–6.

16 Harvey Molotch, 'What do we do with disasters?', *Sociological Inquiry* 84:3 (2014), 370–373 (p. 370).

17 Banet-Weiser, *Empowered*, p. 69.

18 Tiffany Page, Anna Bull and Emma Chapman, 'Making power visible: "slow activism" to address staff sexual misconduct in higher education', *Violence Against Women* 25:11 (2019), 1309–1330 (p. 1321). They cite the case of Sara Ahmed, whose high-profile resignation from Goldsmiths University in 2016 over sexual harassment of students brought much-needed institutional attention to the issue, and raised awareness throughout the UK (p. 1320).

19 Nancy Chi Cantalupo and William C. Kidder, 'A systematic look at a serial problem: sexual harassment of students by university faculty', *Utah Law Review* 2018:3 (2018), 671–786 (p. 672).

20 For a fuller discussion of these dynamics, see Alison Phipps, 'Reckoning up: sexual harassment and violence in

the neoliberal university', *Gender and Education*, DOI: 10.1080/09540253.2018.1482413 (accessed 15 October 2019). I do not have a definitive answer on how institutions should deal with people who perpetrate abuse, and I appreciate that this might be frustrating for readers (although I also think demands for immediate answers can be a way of shutting down critique). I would like feminists working in/on/with institutions to think and talk collectively about alternatives, so that we can learn and grow together.

21  David Batty, Sally Weale and Caroline Bannock, 'Sexual harassment "at epidemic levels" in UK universities', *Observer*, 5 March 2017, https://www.theguardian.com/education/2017/mar/05/students-staff-uk-universities-sexual-harassment-epidemic (accessed 1 November 2019).

22  A very early version of this section appeared as Alison Phipps, 'Whose personal is more political? Experience in contemporary feminist politics', *Feminist Theory* 17:3 (2016), 303–321.

23  For a full discussion of this case, see Alison Phipps, 'Sex wars revisited: a rhetorical economy of sex industry opposition', *Journal of International Women's Studies* 18:4 (2017), 306–320.

24  Holly Davis, 'Defining "pimp": working towards a definition in social research', *Sociological Research Online* 18:1 (2013), 1–15.

25  Mac and Smith, *Revolting Prostitutes*, p. 36.

26  Clare Hemmings, 'Affective solidarity: feminist reflexivity and political tranformation', *Feminist Theory* 13:2 (2012), 147–161 (p. 152).

27  Although Black Lives Matter was started by three Black women – Alicia Garza, Patrisse Cullors and Opal Tometi – many of its supporters have been primarily focused on the deaths of young Black men at the hands of the police.

28  Julia Serano, *Excluded: Making Feminist and Queer Movements More Inclusive* (Berkeley, CA: Avalon Publishing, 2013), p. 31.

29  Cecilia Dhejine, Paul Lichtenstein, Marcus Boman, Anna L. V. Johansson, Niklas Långström and Mikael Landén, 'Long-term follow-up of transsexual persons undergoing sex

reassignment surgery: cohort study in Sweden', *PLoS ONE* 6:2 (2011), 1–8.

30  Amia Srinivasan, 'Does anyone have the right to sex?', *London Review of Books* 40:6 (2018), 5–10, https://www.`lrb.co.uk/v40/n06/amia-srinivasan/does-anyone-have-the-right-to-sex (accessed 1 November 2019).

31  Get the L out!, 'The cotton ceiling', *OBJECT*, https://www.objectnow.org/news/2019/3/29/get-the-l-out-the-cotton-ceiling?rq=Get%20the%20L%20out!%20The%20cotton%20ceiling (accessed 15 October 2019).

32  James Dobson, 'Protect your kids from tyrant Obama', *WND*, 30 May 2016, https://www.wnd.com/2016/05/protect-your-kids-from-tyrant-obama/ (accessed 1 November 2019).

33  Zack Ford, 'Pat McCrory promises retaliation if Charlotte approves LGBT protections', *ThinkProgress*, 22 February 2016, https://thinkprogress.org/pat-mccrory-promises-retaliation-if-charlotte-approves-lgbt-protections-851a66d42fc4/ (accessed 1 November 2019).

34  R. G. Ratcliffe, '"Our daughters" used as the bathroom bill's protection', *Texas Monthly*, 1 August 2017, https://www.texasmonthly.com/burka-blog/daughters-used-bathroom-bills-protection/ (accessed 1 November 2019).

35  S. E. James, J. L. Herman, S. Rankin, M. Keisling, L. Mottet and M. Anafi, *The Report of the 2015 US Transgender Survey* (Washington, DC: National Center for Transgender Equality, 2016).

36  Melissa Gira Grant, 'The war on sex workers', *Reason*, February 2013, https://reason.com/2013/01/21/the-war-on-sex-workers/ (accessed 1 November 2019).

CHAPTER 5

1  Rebecca Traister, *Good and Mad: The Revolutionary Power of Women's Anger* (New York: Simon and Schuster, 2018), p. 17.

2  Michelle Goldberg, 'The Trump resistance will be led by angry women', *Slate*, 22 January 2017, https://slate.com/human-interest/2017/01/the-trump-resistance-will-be-led-by-angry-women.html (accessed 1 November 2019).

# Notes

3 Constance Grady, '2017 was the year of women's anger, onscreen and off', *Vox*, 21 December 2017, https://www.vox.com/2017-in-review/2017/12/21/16776708/2017-womens-anger-womens-march-reckoning-handmaids-tale-alias-grace-big-little-lies-three-billboards (accessed 1 November 2019).

4 Lindy West, 'Yes, this is a witch hunt. I'm a witch and I'm hunting you', *New York Times*, 17 October 2017, https://www.nytimes.com/2017/10/17/opinion/columnists/weinstein-harassment-witchunt.html (accessed 1 November 2019).

5 Ahmed, *Living a Feminist Life*, pp. 210–211.

6 Pankaj Mishra, *Age of Anger: A History of the Present* (London: Penguin, 2017), p. 19.

7 Soraya Chemaly, *Rage Becomes Her: The Power of Women's Anger* (New York: Atria Books, 2018), p. 17.

8 Democracy Now!, 'There are thousands of Cyntoia Browns: Mariame Kaba on criminalization of sexual violence survivors', broadcast 10 January 2019, https://www.democracynow.org/2019/1/10/there_are_thousands_of_cyntoia_browns (accessed 1 November 2019).

9 Lorde, *Sister Outsider*, p. 127.

10 Alison M. Jaggar, 'Love and knowledge: emotion in feminist epistemology', *Inquiry* 32:2 (1989), 151–176 (p. 166).

11 Ahmed, *Willful Subjects*, pp. 15, 165.

12 Arlie Russell Hochschild, *The Managed Heart: Commercialization of Human Feeling* (Berkeley, CA: University of California Press, 1983).

13 Hartman, *Scenes of Subjection*, pp. 34, 144.

14 Anderson, and Samudzi, *As Black as Resistance*, p. 78.

15 Brittney C. Cooper, *Eloquent Rage: A Black Feminist Discovers her Superpower* (New York: St Martin's Press, 2018), pp. 159, 175.

16 Ahmed, *Willful Subjects*, p. 167.

17 Maiysha Kai, 'Ain't I a woman: marching forward – what now?', *The Root*, 24 January 2017, https://www.theroot.com/ain-t-i-a-woman-marching-forward-what-now-1791562448 (accessed 1 November 2019).

18 Anna North, 'The Women's March changed the American

left. Now anti-Semitism allegations threaten the group's future', *Vox*, 21 December 2018, https://www.vox.com/ identities/2018/12/21/18145176/feminism-womens-march-2018-2019-farrakhan-intersectionality (accessed 1 November 2019).

19 Brent Staples, 'How the suffrage movement betrayed Black women', *New York Times*, 28 July 2018, https://www.ny times.com/2018/07/28/opinion/sunday/suffrage-movement-racism-black-women.html (accessed 1 November 2019).

20 Jessica Ringrose and Emma Renold, "F**k rape!' Exploring affective intensities in a feminist research assemblage', *Qualitative Inquiry* 20:6 (2014), 772–780 (p. 775).

21 Black Women's Blueprint, 'An open letter from Black women to the Slutwalk', *Gender & Society* 30:1 (2016), 9–13 (p. 10). Originally published in 2011.

22 Michelle Alexander, 'Why Hillary Clinton doesn't deserve the Black vote', *The Nation*, 10 February 2016, https://www. thenation.com/article/hillary-clinton-does-not-deserve-bla ck-peoples-votes/ (accessed 1 November 2019).

23 Cooper, *Eloquent Rage*, p. 178.

24 Jessie Daniels, 'White women who enable Trump do not deserve the benefit of your doubt', *Huffington Post*, 7 February 2018, https://www.huffpost.com/entry/daniels-opinion-white-women-trump_n_5a79f67de4b0d0ef3c09fbf0 (accessed 1 November 2019).

25 Cooper, *Eloquent Rage*, p. 182.

26 For a full discussion of the idea of white innocence, see Gloria Wekker, *White Innocence: Paradoxes of Colonialism and Race* (Durham, NC: Duke University Press, 2016).

27 Shahida Arabi, '5 powerful lessons Arya Stark teaches us about surviving trauma', *Bitch*, 6 May 2019, https://www. bitchmedia.org/article/arya-stark-lessons-about-trauma (accessed 1 November 2019).

28 Achille Mbembe, 'Necropolitics (translated by Libby Meintjes)', *Public Culture* 15:1 (2003), 11–40.

29 Giorgio Agamben, *Homo Sacer: Sovereign Power and Bare Life*, trans. Daniel Heller-Roazen (Stanford, CA: Stanford University Press, 1998).

30 NAACP, 'Criminal justice fact sheet', https://www.

naacp.org/criminal-justice-fact-sheet/ (accessed 15 October 2019).

31 Terry Gross, '"Times" reporters describe how a paper trail helped break the Weinstein story', broadcast on *NPR*, 15 November 2017, https://www.npr.org/2017/11/15/564310240/times-reporters-describe-how-a-paper-trail-helped-break-the-weinstein-story?t=1571302059472 (accessed 1 November 2019).

32 Sarkar's action was condemned by a group of Indian feminist academics and activists for 'ignoring due process' – this is not the argument I am making.

33 Davis, *Freedom is a Constant Struggle*, p. 142.

34 Natasha Lennard, *Being Numerous: Essays on Non-fascist Life* (London: Verso, 2019), p. 42.

35 Ahmed, *Willful Subjects*, p. 62.

36 Lennard, *Being Numerous*, p. 14.

37 Mbembe, 'Necropolitics', p. 36.

38 David Brown, 'How women took over the military-industrial complex', *Politico*, 2 January 2019, https://www.politico.com/story/2019/01/02/how-women-took-over-the-military-industrial-complex-1049860 (accessed 1 November 2019).

39 Lauren Berlant and Jordan Greenwald, 'Affect in the end times: a conversation with Lauren Berlant', *Qui Parle* 20:2 (2012), 71–89 (pp. 73–74).

40 Cooper, *Eloquent Rage*, p. 198.

41 Arruzza, Bhattacharya and Fraser, *Feminism for the 99%*, p. 4.

CHAPTER 6

1 Ahmed, *Living a Feminist Life*, p. 174.

2 Sofia Lotto Persio, 'Big Lottery fund reviews grant to trans kids charity Mermaids', *Pink News*, 17 December 2018, https://www.pinknews.co.uk/2018/12/17/big-lottery-fund-grant-mermaids/ (accessed 1 November 2019).

3 Paris Lees, 'The life-changing power of Alexandria Ocasio-Cortez and standing together as allies', *Vogue*, 22 February 2019, https://www.vogue.co.uk/article/life-changing-power-of-alexandria-ocasio-cortez (accessed 1 November 2019).

4 Hatewatch Staff, 'The Daily Caller exposed for publishing

prolific anti-Semite: still employs editor with white nationalist ties', 29 May 2018, https://www.splcenter.org/hate watch/2018/05/29/daily-caller-exposed-publishing-prolific-antisemite-still-employs-editor-white-nationalist (accessed 1 November 2019).

5 Madeleine Kearns, 'Feminist testifies against the "Equality Act"', *National Review*, 2 April 2019, https://www.nation alreview.com/corner/feminist-julia-beck-testifies-against-equality-act/ (accessed 1 November 2019).

6 Nick Duffy, 'Radical feminists team up with right wing evangelicals to oppose trans rights protections', *Pink News*, 8 February 2017, https://www.pinknews.co.uk/2017/02/08/radical-feminists-team-up-with-right-wing-evangelicals-to-oppose-trans-rights-protections/ (accessed 1 November 2019).

7 Brynn Tannehill, '"Feminists" who exclude trans women aren't feminists at all', *Huffington Post*, 10 July 2018, https://www.huffpost.com/entry/opinion-tannehill-terfs-right-wing_n_5 b44eeeae4b0c523e2637878 (accessed 1 November 2019).

8 TERF stands for trans-exclusionary radical feminist.

9 Liam Deacon, 'Crowdfunder website shuts down group educating kids about transgender risk evidence', *Breitbart*, 4 June 2018, https://www.breitbart.com/europe/2018/06/04/crowdfunder-shuts-group-educating-kids-transgender-risk-evidence/ (accessed 1 November 2019).

10 R. Totale, 'Bonzo goes to Oslo: Christian fundamentalists and the far right strike a new pose', *Libcom*, 26 February 2019, http://libcom.org/blog/bonzo-goes-oslo-christian-fun damentalists-far-right-strike-new-pose-26022019 (accessed 1 November 2019).

11 Adam Ramsay and Claire Provost, 'Revealed: the Trump-linked "Super PAC" working behind the scenes to drive Europe's voters to the far right', *Open Democracy*, 25 April 2019, https://www.opendemocracy.net/en/5050/revealed-the-trump-linked-super-pac-working-behind-the-scenes-to-drive-europes-voters-to-the-far-right/ (accessed 1 November 2019).

12 Tim Fitzsimons, 'Conservative group hosts anti-transgender panel of feminists "from the left"', *NBC News*, 29 January

2019, https://www.nbcnews.com/feature/nbc-out/conserva tive-group-hosts-anti-transgender-panel-feminists-left-n964 246 (accessed 1 November 2019).

13 In the UK, a small number of anti-fascist groups have recently endorsed trans-exclusionary views.

14 George Monbiot, 'How US billionaires are fuelling the hard right cause in Britain', *Guardian*, 7 December 2018, https:// www.theguardian.com/commentisfree/2018/dec/07/us-bil lionaires-hard-right-britain-spiked-magazine-charles-david-koch-foundation (accessed 1 November 2019).

15 Claire Ainsworth, 'Sex redefined', *Nature* 518 (2015), 288–291. See also Sally Hines, *Is Gender Fluid? A Primer for the 21st Century* (New York: Thames and Hudson, 2018).

16 German Lopez, 'Women are getting harassed in bathrooms because of anti-transgender hysteria', *Vox*, 19 May 2016, https://www.vox.com/2016/5/18/11690234/women-bath rooms-harassment (accessed 1 November 2019).

17 Hatewatch Staff, 'Christian right tips to fight transgender rights: separate the T from the LGB', 23 October 2017, https://www.splcenter.org/hatewatch/2017/10/23/christ ian-right-tips-fight-transgender-rights-separate-t-lgb (acces sed 1 November 2019).

18 Data provided by Ugly Mugs Ireland.

19 Mac and Smith, *Revolting Prostitutes*, p. 149.

20 Charlotte Shane, 'What men want', *Dissent*, spring 2019, https://www.dissentmagazine.org/article/andrea-dworkin-review (accessed 15 October 2019).

21 Laura Agustín, *Sex at the Margins: Migration, Labour Markets and the Rescue Industry* (London: Zed Books, 2007), pp. 37–39.

22 Adam Goldman, 'The Comet Ping Pong gunman answers our reporter's questions', *New York Times*, 7 December 2016, https://www.nytimes.com/2016/12/07/us/edgar-welch-com et-pizza-fake-news.html (accessed 1 November 2019).

23 Mary De Young, *The Day Care Ritual Abuse Moral Panic* (Jefferson, NC: McFarland, 2004).

24 See Arjee Javellana Restar, 'Methodological critique of Littman's (2018) parental-respondents accounts of "rapid-onset gender dysphoria"', *Archives of Sexual Behaviour*,

# Notes

DOI: 10.1007/s10508–019–1453–2 (accessed 15 October 2019).

25 Sara Ahmed, 'You are oppressing us!', *Feminist Killjoys*, 15 February 2015, https://feministkilljoys.com/2015/02/15/you-are-oppressing-us/ (accessed 1 November 2019).

26 Janice Raymond, *The Transsexual Empire: The Making of the She-male* (New York: Teachers College Press, 2004 [1979]), p. 178.

27 Feminists Fighting Transphobia, https://feministsfightingtransphobia.wordpress.com/the-statement/ (accessed 15 October 2019).

28 Flavia Dzodan, 'Greatest hits of Victorian feminism', https://redlightpolitics.info/post/52372119164/greatest-hits-of-victorian-feminism-alien-vs (accessed 15 October 2019).

29 Tweet posted at 9:49 a.m. on 4 February 2019.

30 Hartman, *Wayward Lives*, pp. 370–403.

31 See, for example, Brian Donovan, *White Slave Crusades: Race, Gender and Anti-vice Activism 1887–1917* (Chicago: University of Illinois Press, 2006).

32 Mac and Smith, *Revolting Prostitutes*, pp. 59–60, 75–76.

33 In contrast to their privileged sisters, working-class suffragettes in the UK tended to have a more anti-colonial outlook, and Sylvia Pankhurst was a vocal anti-fascist and anti-colonial activist.

34 Sophie Lewis, *Full Surrogacy Now: Feminism against Family* (London: Verso, 2019), p. 11.

35 Amos and Parmar, 'Challenging imperial feminism', p. 13.

36 Martin Pugh, *Hurrah for the Blackshirts: Fascists and Fascism in Britain between the Wars* (London: Jonathan Cape, 2005), p. 142.

37 Heron Greenesmith, 'Racism in anti-trans "feminist" activism', https://www.politicalresearch.org/2019/02/20/racism-in-anti-trans-feminist-activism (accessed 15 October 2019).

38 Gloria Anzaldúa, *Borderlands/La Frontera: The New Mestiza* (San Francisco: Aunt Lute Books, 1987), p. 19.

39 Martin Belam, 'Toby Young quotes on breasts, eugenics, and working class people', *Guardian*, 3 January 2018, https://www.theguardian.com/media/2018/jan/03/toby-

young-quotes-on-breasts-eugenics-and-working-class-peo
ple (accessed 1 November 2019).
40 Hatewatch Staff, 2017.
41 This dispute was widely reported as 'Muslims versus gays',
despite the existence of anti-LGBT prejudice across all social
groups and the large numbers of LGBT people and allies
from the Muslim community who intervened. There was
also an open letter signed by a number of LGBT individuals
and organisations, highlighting how the dispute had been
weaponised by the government's counter-extremism
strategy in ways that betrayed colonial attitudes that defined
all Muslims as 'backward' and homophobic.

## Conclusion

1 Zillah Eisenstein, *Abolitionist Socialist Feminism: Radi-
calizing the Next Revolution* (New York: Monthly Review
Press, 2019), p. 17.
2 Lorde, *Sister Outsider*, p. 139.
3 Akwugo Emejulu and Leah Bassel, 'Austerity and the politics
of becoming', *Journal of Common Market Studies* 56 (2018),
109–119. See also Akwugo Emejulu and Francesca Sobande,
*To Exist is to Resist: Black Feminism in Europe* (London:
Pluto Press, 2019).
4 Angela Davis, 'Abolition feminism: theories and practices',
lecture delivered at the Nicos Poulantzas Institute, Athens,
11 December 2017, https://mronline.org/2018/01/15/abo
lition-feminism-theories-practices/ (accessed 1 November
2019).
5 Mariame Kaba and Kelly Hayes, 'A jailbreak of the
imagination: seeing prisons for what they are and demanding
transformation', *Truthout*, 3 May 2018, https://truthout.org/
articles/a-jailbreak-of-the-imagination-seeing-prisons-for-
what-they-are-and-demanding-transformation/ (accessed 1
November 2019).
6 Lorde, *Sister Outsider*, p. 111.
7 Lewis, *Full Surrogacy Now*.
8 Ruth Wilson Gilmore, 'Prisons and class warfare: an
interview with Ruth Wilson Gilmore', *Verso Books Blog*,

# Notes

  2 August 2018, https://www.versobooks.com/blogs/3954-prisons-and-class-warfare-an-interview-with-ruth-wilson-gilmore (accessed 15 October 2019).

  9 Gilmore, 'Prisons and class warfare'.

10 Ahmed, 'Declarations of whiteness'.

11 Lauren Michele Jackson, 'What's missing from "white fragility"', *Slate*, 4 September 2019, https://slate.com/human-interest/2019/09/white-fragility-robin-diangelo-workshop.html (accessed 15 October 2019).

12 Lorde, *Sister Outsider*, p. 133.

# Index

# Index

Black feminism (*cont.*)
(NBFO); Olufemi, Lola;
#SayHerName; Smith,
Barbara; #SolidarityIsFor
WhiteWomen; Third
World Women's Alliance;
Truth, Sojourner; Wells,
Ida B.
Black Lives Matter campaign
60, 101, 187 n.27
Black men 15, 50, 53, 99, 125
Black women 39, 116–17, 131,
172 n.2
    marginalisation 14–15,
    89–90, 101, 117–18
    and respectability politics
    115, 118
    sexualisation 50, 53, 73–4,
    118, 145–6
Bolsonaro, Jair 21, 22, 23, 28
boycotts 89–90
Brazil 21, 22, 23, 28
#BringBackOurGirls 88–9
Brownmiller, Susan 42, 44
Bryant, Carolyn 73
Burke, Tarana 2, 13, 35, 37
Butler, Judith 143–4

Cady Stanton, Elizabeth 41
campaigns 1–2, 55, 100, 134,
144
    anti-abortion 137–8
    anti-fascist 127, 193 n.13
    anti-immigration 19–20, 30
    Black Lives Matter 60, 101,
    187 n.27
    Black rights 15, 38, 43,
    51–2, 85
    boycotts 89–90
    petitions 87, 98, 104, 134,
    139
    against pornography 97,
    136–7

against sex work 97–101,
    145–6, 147, 154–5
suffrage 41–2, 117–18, 155,
    194 n.33
against trafficking 98–9,
    154–5
on trans issues 21–6, 104,
    134–5, 138, 142–3, 146
Women's Liberation Front
    (WoLF, USA) 137–8, 139,
    148–9
*see also* hashtags; protests
Canada 28
capitalism 7–9, 17–21, 54–5,
114
    colonial 8, 17, 151–9
    communicative 83, 85, 88,
    91–2
    racial 8–9, 96, 161
Carl, Noah 87, 157
celebrities 1–2, 66, 88–9, 98
censorship 24, 25, 150–1,
157
Chemaly, Soraya 112–13
Chibok schoolgirls
    kidnapping (Nigeria) 88–9
child sexual exploitation
    57–8, 148
CitizenGo (website) 139
Civil Rights movement 38,
    43, 51–2, 85
civility 114–17
class, sex 42, 140, 152–3
class, social 10, 20, 45–6, 72,
    89, 180 n.24
clickbait 92–3
Clinton, Hillary 29, 115, 119
Coalition Against Trafficking
    in Women (CATW) 98–9
Coalition of Immokalee
    Workers 55
colonialism 20, 72–3, 114, 131
    capitalist 8, 17, 151–9

# Index

# Index

justice system *see* criminal punishment system

Kaba, Mariame 58, 163–4
Kavanaugh, Brett 12–14, 31
Kelly, Liz 43
Kendall, Mikki 39

labour *see* sex work; work
Latham, Joanne 104
Latin America 39
legislation 33, 136, 145–6, 158
  gender identity 134, 137–8, 144, 148–9
lesbians 76, 105–6, 134, 151
LGBT people 20–1, 26–7, 29, 75–6, 102–8, 145–6, 158–9
Lorde, Audre 67, 113, 116
lynching 51, 73

MacKinnon, Catharine 45, 64, 97
marginalisation 8, 19–20, 75–6, 115–17, 156–7
  allyship 161, 163, 168–70
  of Black women 14–15, 89–90, 101, 117–18
  and sexual violence 73–5, 79–80
  and trauma 96, 100
May, Theresa 70
Mbembe, Achille 123
McGowan, Rose 39
media 83–5, 90–4, 102, 120–2, 124–5
  *see also* social media
Meili, Trisha (Central Park Jogger) 124
men 9–10, 39–40, 67
  'bad' 47, 77–8, 98, 127
  as victims 66, 69, 77
men's rights activists 27–8, 77, 105

Mermaids (charity) 134–5
#MeToo 1–3, 71, 122–3
  backlash 37–8, 66–8
  and feminists of colour 37–40, 55–6, 77
  impact of 32–3, 35–7, 91–2
Michigan Womyn's Music Festival 102
migration 19–20, 30, 47, 70, 156–7
Milano, Alyssa 2, 35, 36–7, 40, 61–2
Miller, Chanel 78
Miller, Murray 40
Millett, Kate 44, 45
Minassian, Alex 28
misogyny 14–15, 59, 65
moral panic 75–6
Mumsnet 135
music videos 64–5
Muslim women 74–5

naming and shaming 91–2, 122–3, 126
narcissism 61–7, 83, 151
Nassar, Larry 57–8
National Black Feminist Organization (NBFO) 52
National Society for the Prevention of Cruelty to Children (NSPCC) 146
National Women's Law Center 1–2
Native American people 54
necropolitics 129–30, 151
neoliberalism 16–17, 114
news, fake 90–1
niceness 114–15, 117
Nigeria 88–9
no-platforming 150–1
#NoUnexpectedPenises 103

# Index

# Index

# Index

# Index